RULES FOR
RAISING KIDS

RULES FOR RAISING KIDS

By

ROBERT I. LESOWITZ, M.D.

Adult and Child Psychiatry
Canton, Ohio

CHARLES C THOMAS • PUBLISHER
Springfield • Illinois • U.S.A.

Published and Distributed Throughout the World by
CHARLES C THOMAS • PUBLISHER
Bannerstone House
301-327 East Lawrence Avenue, Springfield, Illinois, U.S.A.

© *1974, by* CHARLES C THOMAS • PUBLISHER
ISBN 0-398-03146-0
Library of Congress Catalog Card Number: 74-2204

With THOMAS BOOKS careful attention is given to all details of manufacturing and design. It is the Publisher's desire to present books that are satisfactory as to their physical qualities and artistic possibilities and appropriate for their particular use. THOMAS BOOKS will be true to those laws of quality that assure a good name and good will.

Library of Congress Cataloging in Publication Data
Lesowitz, Robert I
   Rules for raising kids.
   1. Children—Management. I. Title.
HQ769.L389,   649'.1   74-2204
ISBN 0-398-03146-0

Printed in the United States of America
Q-1

FOREWORD

About two years ago I received this book in manuscript, from a psychiatrist, stationed in the Army in Germany. Although we didn't know each other, he has asked me for my comments and if I liked it, could I possibly suggest a publisher. He said he had read my books and thought his ideas were on a similar wavelength. Usually I am sceptical about books that purport to tell you how to raise your kids but I read it and I was intrigued. There was no doubt that Dr. Lesowitz stated very clearly some basic rules that can help anyone a great deal in this most difficult of all jobs, raising children.

Raising kids so that in the end they will like you and you will like them is so difficult in today's society where so many parents and children are dissatisfied with each other. What Dr. Lesowitz has done is to state, in readable language, some basic rules that you cannot only use successfully for raising kids, but everywhere in your life. His very first rule, "Don't fight battles you can't win," makes an awfully lot of sense not only in regard to your kids, but also to your wife, your mother, father, boss and your friends if you want them to stay your friends. He sensibly points out the wisdom of trying not to fight battles at all because even if you win a battle with someone near and dear to you, you may lose the war as many people who have been divorced can certainly testify.

As I read this book, it seemed to me that I used many of these rules in raising my own children, all of whom are grown at the present time. We hardly claim perfection as parents, all we know is that they seem to be happy, they are doing all right as individuals and they are friendly and close to us. We still like being together as a family which I think is a pretty good outcome for this rather chancy business of raising kids. If Dr. Lesowitz' book can help you to make it as a family and as individuals it's well worth reading. As parents, we all need all the help we can get.

WILLIAM GLASSER, M.D.
President
Institute For Reality Therapy
Los Angeles, California

INTRODUCTION

I don't know about you, but I have a terrible time reading books on kids. I keep trying new ones, but usually one of a number of things happens. Frequently I get bored with them and put them down half way through the first or second chapter. If I am able to keep going, I am frequently confused by the big, fancy terms the authors use and I am supposed to know, because I am a psychiatrist. I can imagine how you feel. No two psychiatrists can reach an agreement over the meaning of words like "ego" or "repression." Why on earth use them in a book parents are supposed to be able to understand and get something out of. Another reason I am unhappy with many of these books is that, although the examples they use are interesting, as a parent I have a hard time applying them to my kid and the particular problems I am having with him.

So I have set out to write a book that will not put you to sleep, that will not confuse you or try to impress you with big words, and that will try to give you specific answers for specific problems that you are having with your kid. As you might know, psychiatrists are taught in their residency training to be vague and never to give a direct answer to a direct question. Many of my fellow psychiatrists have favorite expressions such as "aha" or "isn't that interesting." But as parents those comments do not help us much when our "little darlings" are making our lives miserable. As you can probably tell already, much of this book is written by the parent in me because I too have struggled with my kids over the same problems you struggle with; and fortunately I think I found some solutions that work pretty well. I guess I see myself much more as a teacher than a psychiatrist. By that I mean, over the years I have found, as a parent and a psychiatrist, some basic rules that work well in raising kids and I would like to teach them to you.

I believe wholeheartedly in the concept of prevention. With every teenager I see who is in serious trouble, I feel that I can almost always trace it back to many events in childhood, that if handled in a better way, could have prevented this mess I see sitting before me in my office. I must be very honest with you in saying that when kids are seriously in trouble in their late teens and early twenties, there is very little that can be done for them, and the things that can be done are very costly and time-consuming. I guess that is the main reason I went into child psychiatry, because I know that the little problems that arise in childhood, if handled correctly, will not result in bigger problems later in life.

Because I believe wholeheartedly in prevention, I have always been dissatisfied sitting in my office seeing a few families a day. Although I may be helping them prevent problems later on, I cannot help but think about all those people out there that I am not "getting to." That is why I spend a great deal of my time lecturing to large groups of people, for example PTA's and other parents' groups, and am now finally putting my ideas down in book form.

As parents we get even more frustrated when somebody starts telling us about the "unconscious" when we are trying to figure out what to do when our kid has stolen something. We all need answers, and we need them fast. But where do we turn for these answers? Raising kids is a unique experience. Everywhere else in our life to do something we have to take a course and pass a test. For example, to drive a car you do not get out and start driving. You take the course in school or have a relative or friend teach you. You study manuals and pamphlets, and then finally you take a test to see if you are proficient. If you pass, then you get a license and are allowed to drive. But what does it take to be a parent? Unfortunately, to many of us this happens all too easily. Suddenly we wake up one morning, and we find a bunch of kids running around, and they are all calling us "daddy." Where do we turn? Who is going to help us with this mess? To answer these questions we frequently look at how our parents did it with us. Sometimes this works, but frequently it does not. Frequently our own parents bungled things just like we may be bungling things in raising our own kids. Also there is another factor; times have changed from the days of when you could tell a kid to do something and he would do it. Today, all too often, we tell our kids to do something and they quote "Freud" or "Spock" to us. As we all know, the God-like authority that our parents had over us just is not there anymore. That is not bad by the way, but it leaves us without solutions to our problems. It is for these reasons that many of us, as professionals, devote a lot of our time to teaching parent classes and to writing books on how to be a successful parent.

I would like to clarify a common misconception. As psychiatrists working with children we rarely deal with really crazy kids. As a matter of fact, the last time I saw a crazy kid was about five years ago. Mostly, we deal with everyday small problems, that if not handled properly, turn into big problems. The basic rules for raising kids that I have tried to set forth in this book therefore are not only for disturbed kids. I feel that they work with all kids, whether they are normal, troubled, retarded or unusual in some other respect. In other words, these are rules for raising *all* kids.

Finally, let me say that this book is not just for parents, but for anyone who works with kids. Whether you are a parent, teacher, school counselor or juvenile court worker, you need to know how to get kids headed in the right direction and how to curb their bad behavior. The "Rules" apply just as well to behavior in the classroom or the community as they do to behavior at home. Therefore this book will be helpful to anyone who works with kids.

You will get the most out of this book if you read it in its entirety, and in the order you find it. Let us say your kid wets the bed. If you use the book like an encyclopedia and only read Chapter seventeen on bed-wetting, you will not get a good understanding of the problem and what you can do about it. That would be like seeing only the third act of a four-act play. Read through the whole book and then if you wish to re-read a certain problem area, that would be fine. A thorough understanding of the Eight Basic Rules will make it easier for you to understand and deal with the Special Problems discussed in the second part of the book.

ROBERT I. LESOWITZ, M.D.

100-30th Street, N.W.
Canton, Ohio 44709

ACKNOWLEDGMENTS

I would like to thank my former teachers, Doctor Stuart Finch and Doctor Marshal Shearer, who taught me to approach kids' problems with my feet on the ground. I would like to also thank probably my two best tutors, my daughters, Toni and Abby, who have not only taught me mostly what I know of kids, but have frequently taught me the hard way. I would also like to thank my dear wife, Daryl, who made all those "hard days at the office" tolerable.

CONTENTS

RULES FOR
RAISING KIDS

PART I

THE EIGHT BASIC RULES

THESE RULES ARE LIKE GOLF; THE THEORY IS SIMPLE, BUT THE PRACTICE IS MURDER. AS YOU READ OVER PART I, I AM SURE YOU WILL AGREE THE RULES SOUND SIMPLE. AS A MATTER OF FACT, PARENTS ARE USUALLY SHOCKED TO FIND OUT THAT A PROBLEM THEY HAVE BEEN STRUGGLING WITH FOR YEARS HAS SUCH A SIMPLE SOLUTION. BUT THAT IS HOW I FEEL ABOUT GOLF; IT LOOKS SO EASY.

I KNOW IT MAY AT FIRST SOUND SIMPLE TO IGNORE A CERTAIN TYPE OF BEHAVIOR, BUT WAIT TILL YOU TRY IT. YOU WILL FIND IT IS NOT AS EASY AS IT LOOKS. IT IS GOING TO BE TOUGH, AND YOU MAY NEED TO FORCE YOURSELF TO THINK ABOUT IT. IF YOU DO THIS, YOU AND YOUR KID WILL BOTH BE HAPPY.

OCCASIONALLY I SEE A SET OF PARENTS TWO OR THREE MONTHS AFTER THEIR FIRST VISIT AND THEY WILL SAY, "GEE, DOC, WE TRIED YOUR 'RULES' AND THEY DIDN'T WORK." WHEN WE GET DOWN TO THE "NITTY-GRITTY" AND START TALKING ABOUT THEIR "TRYING," I ALMOST ALWAYS FIND OUT THAT THEY TRIED THEM ONCE OR TWICE OR FOR A DAY OR FOR A FEW WEEKS AND, OF COURSE, THEY DID NOT WORK. YOU MUST KEEP IN MIND THAT IF A CHILD HAS A CERTAIN HABIT FOR TEN YEARS AND YOU SUDDENLY CHANGE THINGS IN THE FAMILY, HIS HABITS ARE NOT GOING TO CHANGE OVER NIGHT. THE CHANGE WILL TAKE A LITTLE WHILE. I MUST SAY HONESTLY THAT I HAVE NEVER HAD THE RULES FAIL. I HAVE ONLY HAD PARENTS FAIL AT FOLLOWING THE RULES AND FOLLOWING THEM CONSISTENTLY.

CHAPTER I

RULE 1: *There Are Battles You Can Win and Battles You Can't Win; Never Fight A Battle You Can't Win.*

I am sure you have all heard the expression, "You can lead a horse to water, but you can't make him drink." That saying and Rule 1 have a lot in common. Actually, what you are doing with this rule is admitting to yourself, honestly, that there are certain things in the kid's life you really do not have any control over. Or to put it another way, your kid has absolute control over certain areas of his life. This is hard for us, as parents, to admit because we get very frustrated when we think we cannot control things. We have probably all experienced driving down the road, feeling fairly content, and all of a sudden we hit a patch of ice and start skidding. That tremendous, panicky, frightening feeling is because we suddenly realize we are not in control. Similarly, we get panicky when we realize we cannot control our kids. However, scary or not, we must face the fact honestly that we cannot control certain things. Once you can face that, then you will be in a much better position to deal with these problems.

Keep in mind, when I use the word battles, I am not talking only about fist fights or feuds, or things like that. By the word battles I mean any situation that comes up between parents and child that regularly is a source of hard feelings. For example, if frequently at mealtime Dad and Billy get into it over Billy's not eating his vegetables, that is a battle. It makes no difference whether Dad hits Billy or Billy throws peas at Dad, or they just look at each other with a glare; it is a battle because there are hard feelings between them over the issue of eating.

Let me try to diagram for you how these battles can be broken down into groups. (See page 6.)

We will first discuss the left-hand column, the battles you can't win. There are certain things you get into with your kids that, no matter what you do, you cannot possibly win. Let me give an example. I recently saw a father who was having trouble with his son's not eating meat, and he made up his mind that the kid was going to eat meat. He would take the boy by the back of the neck with his left

5

Table I

BATTLES

Battles You Can't Win	Battles You Can Win	
	Not Worth It	*Worth It*
Potty	Hair-Cuts	Obey the laws
Eating	Clothing	Be in on time
Grades	Smoking	Know whereabouts
Friends		

hand, and with his right hand he would force the meat into the kid's mouth and push it down his throat with his finger. He would then clamp the boy's jaw shut and hold it until the boy swallowed. He would step back and the boy would vomit up the meat all over dad. The point I am trying to make is that if the kid really makes up his mind he is not going to do something, it is almost impossible for us to overcome that. Although there are probably other battles you cannot win, the four I have mentioned (potty, eating, grades and friends) are by far the most common, and they are the greatest source of discontentment in families. I know it may sound ridiculous to you, but when I see a sixteen-year-old kid who has been arrested for shooting or selling heroin, almost always I can trace back with the family to battles that went on as early as age two.

One of these days I am going to write a separate book on the stubborn child because, not only have I struggled with my own stubborn child for years, but I believe they are a separate and difficult entity all to themselves. The reason I mention this is that, particularly with stubborn children, this is an important rule. When you fight battles you cannot win with a stubborn child, you only make him more stubborn. In other words, you cannot make a kid less stubborn by being more stubborn yourself. Frequently when you fight a battle you cannot win, by definition you lose and the child wins, and each time that happens he gets a little tougher. Delinquent children, and particularly teenagers who are in serious trouble, have been fighting battles all their lives with their parents and usually in these battles the parents have not had a prayer of winning.

These four battles are listed in the order they occur because parents usually fight them with their kids at different ages in their lives, potty usually being the first battle. This battle is frequently fought anywhere from one to three years of age and often extends up to age nine, ten or even twenty. In Part II of the book I have devoted a separate chapter to bed-wetting and soiling and, as you will see, these problems are usually the end result of a parent mishandling potty training. In this part of the book I would like to discuss potty training as it applies to Rule 1, since it is most commonly the first battle you can't win.

Neurologists have demonstrated that the bowels and bladder do not have enough nerve endings to begin potty training until the age of one and one half. And many children are not ready till two. If your little boy decided that he was going to wet his pants day and night, and he really made up his mind, is there anything you could do to stop him? You must admit the answer is no. Why not accept it? Why not say to yourself, there is not a thing I can do about it, so why get all upset and get him upset and make everybody miserable? Just let him potty train himself in his own good time. There are some things you can do, like when he is two or two and a half you can buy him a little potty chair to sit on and play with. Sooner or later he will accidentally go in the potty, and you will get all excited and compliment him and praise him. That is not fighting. Remember, I said a battle is regularly a source of hard feelings between parents and kids. If you are praising him, that is not a battle. As you will see in the chapter on bed-wetting and soiling, the only solution for a kid who wets the bed is to make it his responsibility to take care of it and back off, and do not fight with him. The more you fight, the longer the problem will continue. If you walk into his room in the morning and his bed stinks, and you give him a dirty look, that is fighting. If he comes into the house in the afternoon after playing outside and the odor of his pants is enough to boil you over and you holler at him, that is fighting. If you spank him, scold him, grab him, make him feel guilty, all of these things are fighting. Believe me, it is not worth it. All of these kinds of fighting just delay his getting over the problem by himself—because he is in control, not you.

If he already has the problem, you take him aside, and you say, "Look Peter, I know these accidents happen occasionally and I'm not going to get angry about it; however, I would just appreciate it if you would pull down the sheets from the bed if such an accident happens." Or you might say, "Gee, Freddy, when you have an accident in your pants I'd appreciate it if you would rinse them out in the john and throw them over the radiator." Now, if he does not do that, do not go jumping on him because that is fighting, too. You cleaned up messier diapers than that when he was little without complaining too much, and you will probably survive a few more. Just make up your mind that it is something you are going to have to do for a while to help him get over his problem.

The second example of a battle you can't win, and the one that is probably the most needless source of hard feelings in a family, is the battle fought over eating. I am a physician and I could not begin to sit down and figure out exactly what food would be needed for my children, I mean all the calories, vitamins and minerals. How are you as a parent supposed to do that? There are lots of guidelines about eating three square meals per day, and these meals should contain the basic food groups such as starches, meats, vegetables and fats, but they are the averages, and our children at home are not necessarily average. They need a very special diet that is very special for them. You ask, as a parent, how do I figure out what that special diet is? The answer is very simple, you do not.

Let me tell you about an experiment that has been done many times and makes the point very nicely. Take a white laboratory rat who has been raised on regular laboratory rat food all his life. You remove from his diet for two weeks a certain vitamin, like vitamin B_{12}. At the end of two weeks put him in a big cage with ten piles of food of all different kinds and different amounts of vitamins and nourishments, etc. One of these piles is very high in vitamin B_{12}. Automatically the rat will run to the pile that is very high in vitamin B_{12} and eat his fill, and then go on to eat other things. The point is, something in that rat tells him exactly what his body is deficient in and exactly how to make it up. I do not know how that rat even knows that pile is high in B_{12}. All the food smells and tastes about the same. Somehow the rat knows his body needs vitamin B_{12}, and he will make up the deficiency by eating more of it, if left alone.

As dumb as we think our kids are sometimes, you must admit that they are at least as smart as rats. And the same is true for them as for rats. *If left alone, they will eat exactly what their bodies need.*

How should you handle eating? From the time the kid is old enough to point or say a few words (usually age two), you very simply put the food in serving dishes on the table. The whole family comes to the table at the same time, the TV goes off, and people say "pass the mashed potatoes" or whatever they want. If it will make you feel better, you can dish up a little of everything on the plate. From that time on, you say and do nothing about what the kid wants to eat, and you do not fight battles and you do not play games. You do not have to eat your green beans or your spinach to get the dessert. Dessert is part of the meal just like the mashed potatoes and you get that without having to fight any battles or play any games for it. The family members should feel free to talk with each other—after all in our busy society, mealtime is one of the few times when family members can talk with one another. When most of the people at the table are finished eating, mom or dad says "you may be excused" and that is it. You do not have to clean your plate and you do not have to eat your vegetables and you do not have to do a lot of things you do not want to do. You just sit there and eat what your body needs. I have devoted a separate chapter in the second part of the book to eating problems because they are such a common difficulty and a battle you can't win and therefore must not fight.

Like potty and eating I have devoted a separate chapter to school problems. Grades, too, are one of the battles you cannot win and therefore you must not fight. You accept that as being a fact, and you do not try to force kids to get good grades and you do not try and create any hard feelings over grades. You very plainly say to your children when they are young, that if they do well in school, they will probably get a better job and be a little happier. If they fool around in school, it is going to cause them some problems in later life, but after all that is up to them. Of course, you are going to be pleased with them and praise them when they come home with good grades and good report-cards. But you are not going to fight with them if they do not. You are not going to have any battles over their sitting down and doing their homework every night, or your tutoring them, or your punishing them, or buying them off for having a good report card.

My daughter approached me at the dinner table the other night and said, "Say, Dad, did you see my report card?"

I said, "Yes, Toni, that was really very nice, and I'm very proud of you."

She replied, "Well, if you're so proud, don't you think that it is worth about a dollar for each A?"

I replied, "Gee, do you give me a dollar every day I go to work, or do you give Mom a dollar every time she cooks a meal? Of course not.

In a family we all work together, and we each have our certain things that we have to do. I go to work and Mom cooks the meals and you work at school." I continued, "and besides, how are these grades going to help me? They may help you later in life, but they certainly are not going to help me, so why should I pay for them?"

Rewards are just the opposite side of the same coin as punishment and frequently can end up in battles. For example, if you tell a kid you are going to pay him so much for each good grade, sooner or later you are going to have to stop that and, even if it does work for a while, it is going to probably come back in your face when you stop. You may say, "Well, isn't our being pleased with our kids for their good grades a reward?" and I have to agree with you completely. But let's keep rewarding each other with a kind look or a smile, and not the checkbook.

In short, I feel we should leave teaching up to the people that really are supposed to know something about it, the teachers, and leave learning up to the kids. We are going to tell our kids what we expect of them, and we are going to stay interested in their work and how they are doing, but we are not going to fight with them, and we are not going to demand. We are going to admit to ourselves that how they do in school is up to them and we are going to leave them alone to go at it as best they can without creating hard feelings over it.

I am sure you all have heard of Pavlov's experiment where he would ring a bell, give the dog a piece of meat, and the dog would salivate. After doing it repeatedly, he would only have to ring the bell and the dog would salivate. This kind of "conditioned response" happens in our kids all the time. For example, every time Johnny comes home with bad grades he gets spanked, which results in his being angry and upset over school. After a while he does not need to be spanked any more, just the thought of school or the mention of grades will cause him to get angry and cause him to respond to school in an angry way. So he drops out the day he turns sixteen and everybody loses.

The fourth and final battle you can't win is the battle many people have, particularly with their teenagers, over their friends. A mother came to me last year and said, "Dr. Lesowitz, my daughter is only fourteen years old and she is going with a boy who is a bad influence on her. I have been trying to break them up and I have not been able to do it. What would you suggest?" I tried to explain to this mother about battles you can win and battles you cannot win, but after about forty-five minutes I saw I just was not getting anywhere. She shook her head violently and said she just could not be a party to sitting back and letting her daughter run around with that "bum." I said I could appreciate how she felt and I would not like it if it were my own daughter, but I really did not know what she could do about it. I further suggested that she just back off and encourage *her daughter* to make the decisions about who her friends were going to be. When she got up to angrily storm out of my office, I tried to remind her that all the girl had to do to make sure she kept her boyfriend was to get pregnant. But mother told me that was nonsense and reminded me that the girl was only fourteen years of age. You probably know the rest of the story already, and it is a sad one that happens all too often. Three months later I got a call from this mother who was crying over the phone. She said she needed to see me because her daughter was pregnant, and she needed some help.

If kids want to see a friend badly enough, they are going to find a way, even if they have to get pregnant, or run away, or skip school or lie to you. Your kid's having a friend who is a bad influence on him is problem enough. Do you have to force other problems onto your kid such as running away or lying?

We have talked about the four big battles you can't win: potty, eating, grades and friends, and I have asked you to accept certain things as being true, that is, that these are battles you cannot win and therefore are battles you should not fight.

On the other hand, I would like to give you some examples of battles you can win. As you noticed earlier, I have broken that category down into battles you can win but are not worth it and battles you can win that are worth fighting.

Did you ever know anybody who died of long hair? I did not. We all have some funny ideas about kids with long hair, who tend to use drugs or get into certain kinds of troubles, but it is not the long hair that causes them to do that. They are problem children and sometimes one of the things they do along with taking drugs is growing long hair. But it is not the hair that is illegal. I saw a tragic case not too long ago that comes to my mind when I talk about problems with haircuts. One afternoon an army sergeant came to see me and was quite upset about his two sons, aged sixteen and eighteen, who had been arrested for trafficking in drugs. He could not bring his boys in to see me because they refused and mother was "too upset" to come. He sat there over the next hour and told me about their current problem and, when I asked him about past problems he and the boys regularly fought over, he said their biggest fight had always been over haircuts. Dad's hair, by the way, was a very, very short flat top with "white sidewalls." You can see, he was overly concerned with haircuts. But just because we have a hang-up, that does not mean we should impose it on our children. If anything, when we have a hang-up we have to be super careful that we do not impose it on the rest of our family. This father told me how, over the years, he had fought with his two boys over and over again about haircuts, and the more he fought the longer their hair got. Finally, after years of fighting, he developed a new approach. He would hide behind the door, and when they would come in the house, he would jump them, wrestle them to the floor and cut their hair himself. Obviously, after years and years of hard feelings, the resentment became so great that the boys went out and started trafficking in drugs and were eventually arrested. What a beautiful way to get back at the old man! This is an extreme case, but I mention it to make a point—you can create so many hard feelings fighting over little things, and these hard feelings can lead to disaster. The haircut business fits into this category because, although it is a battle you can win, I certainly do not recommend fighting it because it just creates hard feelings. Very similar to this, is the problem of dress; after all they do not ask us to dress that way, but we should be able to tolerate it in them. This is a battle you can win, but it is not worth all the hard feelings.

Another issue which I prefer to include under this category of battles you can win but are not worth it is the battle in some families over smoking. Here you may tend to disagree with me when I say it is not worth it. I smoked for many years myself, but I quit because I honestly believed that smoking was a danger to my health. I certainly encourage my children not to smoke. I try to teach them everything I can about the dangers of smoking, but further I have elected not to fight with them over it and not to create the game-playing and hard feelings that go along with it. If they want to smoke, they are going to, even if they have to hide from me and I would rather they did not have to sneak around. In short, the approach I have taken with my children, and recommend strongly is that you sit down with your kids when they are six, seven or eight and can understand, and you explain to them the many dangers of smoking, but you end the conversation by saying, "But after all they are your lungs and it's your body and what you want to do with it is up to you." That is worrisome for us parents. We feel we are not in control, and we get a little panicky, but let's face it—if left alone kids really make very excellent decisions. Our problem is we just cannot leave them alone and let them make their decisions. We always have to threaten and coerce and bug and harass. Do not do that.

The last category of battles I would like to mention are the battles you can win and are worth fighting. Sometimes people mistakenly get the impression that I am permissive or lenient. Nothing could be farther from the truth. As a matter of fact, I think I am one of the strictest parents I have seen, and I see parents all day long. I like to think I am strict in a reasonable way, that is, strict concerning things I can have some say over. This is what I mean by battles you can win and are worth it. It is essential that you encourage as well as demand that your children obey the law. You would not think of letting them drive a car when they are fourteen nor would you encourage them to break the law in other ways. In fact as parents, although it is very painful for us, we sometimes have to "turn our own kids in" when they have done something wrong, and we should. This teaches them that you respect the law and, no matter how much it bothers you to see it happen, you will make sure that they will obey the law. Whenever I use the term "law" I do not mean mom's law or dad's law, I mean the generally accepted laws of the land and laws of the community. For example, there are state laws that say kids must go to school until they are sixteen, and those are the laws I am talking about. I do not mean that dad is allowed to get away with saying, "In this house it is my law that your hair will not come down below your collar."

The second area that I think is important is that parents must agree on what time their kids should be in the house and must follow through and make sure that happens. It certainly is a battle you can win; you can track them down and drag them home if need be, and I think you should. Hopefully, it will be a reasonable time, and again, let me emphasize that it should be a time that mom and dad agree on. This time should be very clearly stated to the kids. For example, I see many parents that tell their kids that they have to be in "when it is dark." But what does that mean? What looks dark to me may look like twilight to somebody else and may look like daylight to a third party. Make it something that has no room for interpretation, like, "Be home at eight o'clock."

Lastly, I think it is important for parents to always know where their children are. That does not mean you should always have a say over it, or that kids even should have to ask every time they want to go some place, but it does mean that generally we should know about where they are. Kids do seem to get into less trouble when they have to keep their parents informed as to their whereabouts. If you make a rule that they will keep you informed and they break it, of course some restriction will have to follow. But after all, this is a battle you can win and it is worth fighting.

If you have a wife that bugs you, you will probably know first hand what happens. After hearing this constant "yakking" you just automatically become deaf to it. You just turn her off. That is how it is with kids whose parents fight a lot of battles with them, particularly those who fight battles they cannot win and who fight battles that are not worth it. They just hear their parents bug them about so many things that, after a while, they just turn them off completely and do not hear the really important things their parents have to say. It is so much better if you can leave most of the decisions to your children and only lay down the rules on the really important things. You will have a much better chance of them hearing you if you do it that way.

CHAPTER II

RULE 2: *Always Follow Through and Be Consistent: Don't Make A Threat You Can't Keep.*

Picture in your mind for a moment a wild horse in a large circular corral. The horse is going to spend a great deal of his day walking the length of that fence searching for openings in it, and when he finds one, he is going to go through it. Such is the case with our kids and the rules and limits we set for them. They are constantly trying to find inconsistencies and openings in the rules and trying to get away with things. For example, if dad puts the kid on restriction for a week and the kid knows mom can be worked on, he will probably do it. He will probably start by going to mom with a very sad look on his face and saying how bad he feels about the whole business and wouldn't it be nice if he could get off early to go to the show. At that point, if mom lets the kid off after five days instead of seven days, not only has she blown any value to the restriction, but she has taught the kid that he can cheat the system. This is in fact, as you will see later in the chapter on delinquency, how we sometimes accidentally encourage our kids to be dishonest and cheat the system. We show them the system has lots of holes in it they can squeeze through, and then we proceed to let them do it.

Let's face it; we all have a tendency to want to get away with things, particularly, rules that are laid down for us by somebody else. You can best prevent your kid from getting away with things and also prevent him from developing the habit of getting away with things and of trying to cheat the system by making sure all the gates are closed. To put this in specific terms, *everybody in the kid's life should be doing the same thing with him.* When I work in schools, for example, most frequently I will sit down with everybody in the kid's life except the kid, including the parents, the teachers, and if there are other important people in the family situation, I will include them. If perhaps the minister, the school counselor or the assistant principal has been involved a great deal in the child's behavior, I will get him to join us. Grandparents are very frequently involved in the problem some way. All too often I hear that mom and dad are trying very hard to change their kid's behavior and the grandparents come along and undo it. Frequently, if the grandparents are living with the family, it is important to get them in on the conferences too. The point of all this "togetherness" is that I feel it is important for everybody in the child's life to be doing the same thing with him. If we do not do the same thing, we will have to pay the price for it somehow, and usually that somehow is by the kid's manipulating the system, using somebody who has not been tuned in to the problem.

I remember all too well several years ago having a problem with my own daughter that taught me this lesson the hard way. I was trying to teach my youngest daughter to be more mature and responsible by giving her more responsibility. When she would ask for help in tying her shoes or in dressing herself, my wife and I agreed that we would ignore her. We would give her one of those "you-must-be-kidding" looks. I know this is ordinarily an approach that works, but it just was not working with my own kid. I had a rude awakening several weeks later when I was home sick in bed on the day the cleaning lady came. This old grandmotherly-type gal came into the house and for the next seven hours proceeded to treat my daughter as if she were a helpless infant. She dressed her, tied her shoes and even fed her. Of course my daughter loved every minute of it. My daughter was doing a fantastic job of manipulating this gal and getting her to wait on her hand and foot. There is an infant in all of us who would love to be taken care of and cuddled and bathed and fed and stroked, but few of us, especially in our adult years, can get away with that. But there was my five-year-old daughter acting perfectly helpless and getting this woman to wait on her.

There was the answer to the mystery right before me. The rest was simple. I took the cleaning lady aside and insisted she not baby my daughter. Once I was able to get her to join the team, the problem with my daughter very quickly disappeared.

The word consistency has several important meanings. It means that everybody in the child's life should be doing the same thing, and it also means the child's problems should be handled about the same way each time.

I was asked to see a seven-year-old boy who was constantly in fights in the classroom, on the playground and in the neighborhood. When talking with the boy he seemed like a very happy, healthy, normal young lad, and I did not see any explanation for his fighting. Then I talked to the parents. I asked them what their attitude was toward fighting, and they gave me pretty much the pat middle-class answer,

"We don't want him to start fights, but we want him to defend himself when somebody else fights with him." This is all very interesting and sounds as American as mom's apple pie, but I think for the most part it is a dangerous approach to take with kids. What do you consider "starting it"; a push, a shove, a nasty word, a hit? The kid is almost left to his own devices to decide when to fight. But on top of it, the real problem was that sometimes dad would spank him for fighting, sometimes he would holler at him, sometimes he would confine him to his room and sometimes he would accidentally reward him for his fighting. The rewards came in a subtle kind of way. When the boy would be fighting with his big brother and would haul off and sock him in the belly making the older kid double over, father would sit back and smile with pride at what a great job that was. Parents' pleasure is one of the greatest rewards in the world and probably one of the strongest motivating factors for little kids. The big problem there was consistency. To complicate the matter further mom was trying other sorts of punishment, and still further the boy's grandmother would sit back and smile when he got into fights and say, "My, isn't he all boy." Not only was everybody in the family expecting different things of this boy, but they were all trying to modify his behavior in different ways at different times. For this particular case the solution was very simple. Everybody in the family and school had to get together and decide that this boy's fighting was getting him into a lot of trouble and was going to stop, and stop completely. No fighting, whether the boy starts it or somebody else starts it. Further, everytime the school became aware of the boy's fighting they were to notify the parents. And anytime the parents became aware of the boy's fighting, they were to punish him (not reward him, but punish him) and do it in a consistent and regular way.

There is one very common mistake about this word consistency. The mistake is that parents interpret it to mean they have to treat all the kids the same way. Consistency does not mean that. Kids are different. They are born different and they stay different and they need to be handled differently. What works for one kid will not work for another. The goal is to "tailor-make" the rewards, controls and disciplines that will work well for each kid. One child in the family may need scolding for a certain act whereas another child may need to be ignored. This entirely depends on the kid and why he is doing some of the things he is doing.

Let me mention briefly the second part of Rule 2, that is, "Don't make a threat you can't keep." How often while walking through a supermarket do I hear a mother threaten, "If you don't stop touching that stuff, I'm never going to take you shopping again!" Isn't that ridiculous? If she would think about it, she would not make that statement. It is very unlikely that she is never going to take him shopping again. What she probably means is that, "If you don't stop touching that, I'm not going to take you shopping for a week or two." This may sound like no big deal to you, but it is important. It is important for the reason that kids should listen to what we parents say. One of the biggest complaints of parents is that their kids do not listen to them. But after all, we accidentally teach them not to listen to us. The mother in the supermarket made an unrealistic threat she could not stick to and sooner or later she will have to back down. The kid learns not to listen because he knows mom will not stick to her threats. I think most of us want our children to listen carefully to what we tell them, and one way to accomplish that is by being more careful about our threats.

You would be surprised to know how many parents make very frightening threats, such as "I'm going to kill you," or, as my father used to say to me, "I'm going to peel you like a banana." Sometimes these threats sound funny to us, but children fail to see the humor in it. They take it very realistically and think we really are going to kill them, and may become unreasonably frightened about the threat. Fear is not a reasonable way to modify kids' behavior.

CHAPTER III

I would like to teach you about the concept of reinforcement. Although I promised you in the introduction of this book that I was going to stay away from big words that even the professionals cannot agree on, this word "reinforcement" is something I think most everybody in the business would agree on. The concept is very simple. In short, if your kid does something well and you praise him for it, he is probably going to do it again. If your kid does something and you react as if you are pleased with him, he is going to repeat it. If your kid does something and you let him know that you are not pleased or you ignore it, then he probably will not do that again.

Let me give you an example. Let us suppose that one day I am walking across the floor in my office and I trip over my big feet and I stumble, hitting my head on the wall. Just at the moment when my head hits the wall, some gold coins drop out of the ceiling. You do not have to think very long about what I am going to do next; I am going to keep banging my head on the wall as long as the gold coins keep coming. Probably every day, when I come into my office, I am going to at least bang my head a few times and get some more gold coins. Let us suppose one day when I come into my office after many months of doing this, I bang my head on the wall and no gold coins come out of the ceiling. I will probably bang a few more times just to make sure, but after a while I will probably stop.

Kids are very much this way too. As long as they are doing something that is working for them, that is, as long as they are getting something out of their behavior, they are going to continue to do it, just like, as long as those gold coins kept falling I would continue banging my head. Where we parents get messed up with our kids is that we do not recognize which are the rewards (gold coins) and which are the punishments. Suppose your child is two years old and right now he wants some attention. As typical with two-year-olds, one good way to get attention is by having a temper tantrum. He throws himself on the floor, cries and screams, bangs his fists and bangs his head on the floor. Well, you are not going to sit back and let this kid push you around, so you jump up and grab him and spank his bottom. Let us take a look at this sequence of events more carefully. The child wanted attention. You reacted to him thinking you were punishing him. But were you really punishing him? No, not at all. As a matter of fact, you have just rewarded him (or given him some gold coins) because he was trying to get your attention and he got it. You probably never thought spanking is a reward, but it is just that in many cases. Not only spanking, but hollering, hitting, dirty looks, etc. are frequently rewards because they are paying attention to the kid's behavior and that is exactly what he wants. At this point you are probably asking, but what else is there? There is only one answer to that and that is, *the behavior should be ignored.*

In the example above I tried to explain to you how we "accidentally" reward our kids' bad behavior. Although we have the best intentions in the world, very frequently we reward bad behavior and therefore it continues.

Remember, I said in the beginning of this book that raising kids is like playing golf, the theory is easy, but the practice is murder. Right now we are into a beautiful example of this problem. This theory is very simple. Good behavior should be praised, and bad behavior should be ignored. Certainly, if the behavior reaches that point where it can no longer be ignored, you will have to stop the child or put him in a place where he can be ignored, for example, in the corner of his room. Many parents at this point are probably feeling, "This guy, Lesowitz, is turning out to be another one of those permissive headshrinkers." Nothing could be farther from the truth. I am only trying to get you not to accidentally reward your kid's bad behavior.

What did I mean when I said, "when it reaches the point where it can no longer be ignored?" Obviously this very much depends on each specific situation. If my two kids are in their bedroom fighting with one another, they are probably doing it to get my attention, so I certainly will not go in there and break it up or say anything. However, if one is chasing the other one down the hall with a knife, she has reached that point where "it can no longer be ignored," and then I am going to have to stop her. Stopping her does not mean beating up on her, it means stopping her; taking the knife away and putting her in her room until she cools off and can come out without having to do that sort of thing again.

When my two daughters were small, because they were close in age, they fought with each other constantly. It got on our nerves, and my wife and I found that we were constantly refereeing a fight or an argument, and we were both fed up with it. One day I came home from work and walked in the front door, and to my surprise, my kids were playing in the other room with their dolls, just having a great time and getting along very well together. My wife was downstairs doing the laundry. A few seconds after my kids heard me walk in, they suddenly started fighting with each other, which was more the custom. I was really puzzled by this, so I turned around and went down to talk to my wife about it. It was almost as if this was my kids' way of saying, "Hi, Dad, come on in here and get involved with us." In other words, they were saying "pay attention to us."

As my wife and I talked about this, it was almost as if somebody suddenly turned the lights on. I could see how over the years their fighting was mainly for attention and every time my wife or I broke it up, or refereed, we were actually rewarding rather than punishing their behavior. Even though at times I had spanked, hollered and hit, all these times were reinforcing or rewarding the bad behavior. It seemed logical, therefore, that there was only one solution; just ignore the fighting. At that point my wife and I made up our minds that from then on we were going to ignore the fighting completely. We were not going to get involved with the name-calling, harassing, the fighting or even the hitting. Of course, the only exception to that being that we would get involved if the situation was life-threatening. For years now, things have been delightfully peaceful. Occasionally there are little disagreements, but there is a complete change over the days when the bickering was constant and continuous.

Essentially what I have shown you in this example is that, when my kids' behavior stopped getting them something, that is, when it did not get them attention any more, they gave it up.

Our kids do a lot of things for attention. Probably a lot more than we recognize. It always amazes me when a psychoanalyst gets so caught up in the "whys." One of my old professors gave me some very good advice when he told me to remove that word "why" from my vocabulary when I am working with kids. We do not have to dig down into their unconscious or into their earlier childhood to find out the whys. Mostly kids do something because they want attention, and they want it constantly. That is true with adults too. We need attention, but we have, hopefully, learned socially acceptable ways of getting it. For example, if one day I was home and I wanted some attention from my wife, I could walk up to her and smack her in the mouth. That would surely get her attention, but it would probably not be the kind of attention I was looking for. On the other hand, if I sort of snuggled up to her or gave her a hug in the kitchen, she would probably pay me some attention and probably the kind that I like. It is the same with our kids, except they have not always learned the good ways of getting it because sometimes we have accidentally taught them that the bad ways of getting attention work just as well, if not better.

Kids are like little bookmakers; they play the odds. Let us suppose that little seven-year-old Johnny is sitting at home one day and he is feeling in the mood for attention. He is kind of thinking to himself, "Boy, I haven't had any attention for a long time and I really am hungry for some. Now, let me see. If I walk out there in the living room where mom and dad are sitting, and I act like a good, sweet little boy, is that going to get me attention? Well, probably about a twenty percent chance. But on the other hand, if I walk out there and pick up mom's favorite vase and smash it on the floor, that'll get me attention for sure. There is a hundred percent chance I'll get attention that way."

This is what I meant when I said kids play the odds. And the odds are much more certain, unfortunately, that bad behavior will get noticed whereas good behavior may not. When you go to see your family doctor, he does not tell you all the things that are right with you, he tells you what is wrong. Or the garage mechanic does not tell you what is working on your car and the traffic cop does not tell you how well you drove for the last few days. No, our society is based, all too often, on what people do wrong instead of what they do right. Perhaps this works out okay for the traffic cop or the garage mechanic, but it does not work out for us in raising kids. We must, as parents, pay attention to what the kids do right and play down the things they do wrong. If we do not, we are likely to accidentally reward bad behavior. In other words, if you want your kid to behave well, make the odds a hundred percent that his good behavior will get recognized and his bad behavior maybe will only get recognized five percent of the time. Then there will be no question of how he will try to get your attention, by being good.

Let us look at some other common examples. How often, when your kid hands you one of his school test papers, do you say, "Oh, you got ten wrong?" Would it not be much better to say, "Very good, Jimmy, you got ninety right."?

Another common example that demonstrates the point beautifully, I think, is stuttering. For years and years speech people have been doing research on stuttering to try to understand why it occurs. There are many different thoughts about this, but one thing is certain; in the family of a child who goes on to stutter a great deal, somebody always reacts to it and pays attention to it. All kids stutter at one time or another, usually very briefly. The difference between the kid who stutters briefly and the kid who goes on to stutter for a lifetime is how much attention is paid to it, usually by his parents.

A few years ago one of my daughters walked into the room at dinnertime and started talking, and the words came out with a terrible lisp. Every time she would start to say anything her tongue would get in the way, and she would stumble over it. At that moment I literally grabbed my wife and hurried her off into the kitchen, pretending to take a look at the roast. When we got in there, I explained to my wife about kids' stuttering and that, if we ignored it completely, I promised it would go away in a matter of a few days. That is exactly what happened. My daughter stuttered and lisped occasionally for the next few days, and then the problem disappeared and has never returned. If I had rewarded her stuttering by paying attention to it, either by scolding or commenting or whatever, it probably would have continued.

There are millions of things like this that kids do. Most kids steal at one time or another. But it seems that kids who go on to steal repeatedly have lots and lots of attention paid to their stealing, rather than a simple, "Hey, kid, we don't do that."

It is almost as if kids are constantly on the lookout for new and different things that will rattle our cages. Sometimes they try crying and whining and lisping and even facial twitching. If they "don't work," then the kids give them up. If they do, the behavior continues. If you happen to know of a kid who whines or cries a great deal, just find out what his parents do when the kid does that. I will bet you anything that they do not ignore it. They react to it one way or another, which only encourages the behavior to continue.

The last point I would like to make about this business of reinforcement is that just because you have changed does not mean that the kid is going to change right away. Remember when I was telling you about banging my head on the wall until one day the gold coins stopped? Even though the gold coins stopped falling, I still continued to bang my head a few more times just to make sure that the coins really were not going to come anymore. So it is with kids. Even though you suddenly stop accidentally rewarding their bad behavior, they are probably going to try it a few more times, just to make sure that there are not going to be any rewards coming. Also keep in mind that everytime you slip and react to bad behavior, the kid's progress is going to back-slide. If you decide that a certain behavior needs to be ignored, work very hard at it. Do not ignore for a while and then react and then ignore again. This will not bring you the results you want. You must consistently reward good behavior and ignore bad.

CHAPTER IV

RULE 4: *Don't Put Up Roadblocks To Kids' Feelings, Especially Anger.*

While discussing the last rule, I was telling you how, all too often, parents, doctors and other people get caught up in looking at all the things that are wrong, instead of the things that are right. I got interested a few years ago in looking at families that were pretty successful. I do not mean that in a financial way, but successful as far as raising their kids and having their kids grow up happy and healthy and well-adjusted. What I consistently found when interviewing the parents of kids who have grown up well was something unusual. The kids were encouraged to express anger.

In most of the families I see there are a lot of feelings that do not get expressed, especially angry feelings, or at least they do not get expressed in "reasonable" ways. In "successful families," however, when parents are mad at their kids, they let them know about it directly. When the kids are mad at their parents, they let them know directly

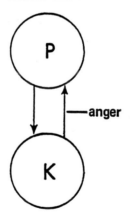

Figure 1. Successful way of expressing anger.

too. Figure 1 represents these "successful families." The P is for parents, the K is for kid, and the arrows represent anger.

Whenever I say express anger directly, always keep in mind that I mean, not only directly but appropriately. In other words, if the father in one of these successful families was mad at his kid for, say,

25

breaking a dish, he would not throw himself on the floor, cry and scream and bang his fists and have a temper tantrum. That would not be appropriate. He would express his anger directly and appropriately and perhaps raise his voice and look angry and say "be more careful" or "stop breaking dishes." This would be appropriate.

Likewise, when the kid of a "successful family" is mad at his parents, he lets them know directly and appropriately also. For example, one of these kids, angry at his father for punishment, might say in a loud tone of voice, "Dad, I get really mad at you when you make me stand in the corner."

This probably all sounds well and good, until you give it a little bit more thought. Is this how it really works in your family? Probably not. Probably you do okay on the first part of it, that is, mom and dad's getting mad at the kids. But where most of us parents fall down, is when it comes time for the kids to get mad at us. Then we become hypocrites; it is all right for us to get mad at them, but "they better not talk back to me." How come? Are we that sensitive as parents that we are going to fall apart if our kid says an angry word to us? I really doubt that. As a matter of fact, it is pretty hard to understand why we do not let our kids talk back to us or express anger. Probably there is no logical reason for it except that, that is just how our parents did it with us.

We have talked about how they do it in "successful families" where people express their anger directly and appropriately, whether they are kids or adults. But how about other families? Let us take a look at what we can call the "unsuccessful family," or the family that does not really make it, as far as having their kids grow up happy and healthy with a minimum number of hang-ups.

In Figure 2 you can see what happens with many families. There is a big, thick wall up between the parents and the kid. This is a funny kind of wall; it is like a two-way mirror. The parents can get their anger through it easily to the kid, but when it comes time for the kid to get mad at his parents directly, the wall stops him. What are the alternatives?

Many of us tend to believe that, if you are mad and you do not say something, the anger will probably go away. Nothing could be farther from the truth. *Anger kept inside does not disappear.* It just lies there and causes problems. Take a look at Figure 3.

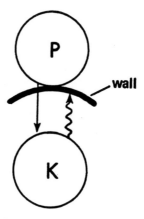

Figure 2. Road block preventing kid from expressing anger.

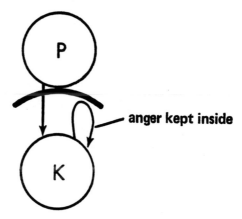

Figure 3. Anger kept inside.

The arrow on the left represents parents anger towards the kid, and that one is not stopped by the wall. The arrow on the right is an example of trying to keep anger inside, or in other words, because the kid cannot get mad at his parents, the anger bounces back on himself. Kids who keep angry feelings inside frequently are withdrawn. depressed and very often have what we call "psychosomatic problems." These are problems that start out mentally and end up physically. For example, if a man is under a lot of pressure at work, his problem certainly starts out emotionally. He is upset and tense and nervous. But after a while of keeping his angry feelings inside, stomach acid starts dripping away and he develops an ulcer. There is nothing imaginary about an ulcer; it is real and it is painful. This is probably one of the most common examples of a psychosomatic problem. There are many more psychosomatic problems, particularly ones that occur in children. For example, the hundreds of eight-year-old boys that I have seen who have been forced to keep their angry feelings inside and tend to walk around depressed and withdrawn. Most frequently they have difficulty with nausea and vomiting, stomachaches, and even diarrhea. The list of psychosomatic problems in kids who are forced to keep their feelings inside is very long. It ranges from ulcerative colitis, asthma and eczema to headaches, stomachaches and, sometimes, violent nightmares. All of these problems (in part) start out mentally and end up physically.

The second thing that can happen with anger if it does not get expressed directly is for the kid to try and express it indirectly (see Fig. 4). Frequently this indirect way is so roundabout and subtle that we parents do not even realize the kid is getting back at us. The most common example I see is a child, with normal intelligence, who is doing poorly in school. Frequently I find out that the parents do pretty

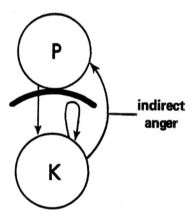

Figure 4. Unsuccessful ways of expressing anger.

well as far as getting angry at the kid, but when it comes time for the kid to get angry at the parents, that is a no-no. Remember what I said before about anger that is kept inside not disappearing? In this case the kid gets back at his parents indirectly. He does badly in school which certainly hurts his parents.

Two things are particularly bad about this "unsuccessful" system of expressing anger. First of all, if a kid is angry at his parents, he wants to make them hurt a little bit. This is a normal reaction for any of us. We express anger by making somebody else hurt a little. But the kid who tries this indirect (unsuccessful) method is always going to hurt himself more than he hurts his parents. The girl who goes out and gets pregnant, to get back at her mother, is really hurting herself much more than her mom. Or the boy who gets arrested for selling dope is hurting himself much more than he is hurting his father. The second thing is that these patterns of behavior become habits, and most frequently we keep these habits for a lifetime. In Figure 4, you could erase the P and put in husband or other significant people in the kid's life, and the kid will tend to react the same way toward them as he did toward his parents.

I used to do a lot of marriage counseling and very frequently I would find that a couple was doing a very bad job of expressing their anger appropriately. For example, the wife might tend to keep all her feelings inside and sulk and walk around depressed. In talking with this wife, though, I would almost always find out that, as a child, she had the same kind of relationship with her parents. Only then it was different, in that her parents were forcing her to keep her anger inside, whereas perhaps today, her husband is not. But nevertheless, because the habit was formed very early in life and was kept up for many years, it continues to be a problem for her, even in her married life.

You can see that Figure 4 represents unsuccessful ways of trying to handle anger. We all know our kids learn very early how to get back at us and how often I have heard that expression from a parent, "Boy, he really knows how to get me where I live." That is certainly true. They know exactly where our sensitive areas are and where our weak spots are and exactly what to say and do to drive us up the wall. And when they use these indirect approaches of anger, they always hit us in our weak spots. In our middle class society most of us share similar concerns. We want our kids to get a good education, and we want them to stay out of trouble (which usually means delinquency for boys and pregnancy for girls). These are our weak spots. Is it any wonder then that these are the two most frequent areas kids tend to use to get back at us? As if it were not easy enough for our kids to learn where our weak spots are, all too often we advertise our weak spots to them. For example, we come home all panicky about dope and start preaching and hollering and giving lectures on not using drugs. By getting that upset about something, we just advertise it as a weak spot to our children. We do this when we overreact about anything. If the kid steals something and you say calmly to him, "Hey, we don't do that; it's wrong," and further you have him return it to the store where he took it and see the manager (all the time keeping calm), probably it will not happen again. But suppose you catch him stealing and get upset about it and hit and holler and carry on; that is just like holding up a sign to your kids saying, "Stealing is my weak spot." Kids find out our weak spots easily enough without us advertising them.

I would like to comment a little bit more on the wall you see in Figure 4. Most parents feel that there is a wall up in their family but do not know exactly how it got there. Frequently they blame the kids for it. There are probably as many different ways to put a wall up as there are parents. For example, my father did it by saying, "You can't talk back to me," just as his hand came crashing across my face. My mother put a wall up in a very different, but just as effective way. Frequently when I tried to get mad at her, she became tearful. That sure shut off my anger.

Walls get put up frequently by parents not being there, whether it be because of a divorce, separation or work which takes parents away from the home a great deal. Sometimes parents just find it easier to get out of the house than sit around and hear somebody get angry at them. Many parents, especially fathers, play the game of ostrich all too often. They stick their heads in the sand so they do not have to hear or see the anger that their kids are feeling for them. There are many ways to do this; the most common is getting buried in the television set, or a good book, or the workshop in the basement, or even the neighborhood bar or bowling alley. The fact of the matter is, unfortunately, that if you are not there, your kid cannot get angry at you, and he is probably going to end up taking out that anger in some other more self-destructive way.

Perhaps as you are reading this section on anger, you are saying to yourself, "Gee, we've got a wall up in our family. What can we do about it?"

The first place to start is to take that wall down. You can do this in two ways. First of all, you sit down with the kids and you say something like, "You know kids, I just read something interesting that made me realize we've been doing some pretty strange things in our family and maybe some things that are pretty unfair. You know, when I am mad at you I let you know about it, usually by hollering at you or something. But how about when it's time for you to get mad at me? You don't do it. And you don't get mad at me because I usually don't let you. That doesn't seem very fair to mom and me any more. We think that, if it's fair for us to get mad at you, then it's fair for you to get mad at us. From now on, when you are sore at mom or me, we'd like you to come to us and tell us about it, and I promise you that we're not going to get all upset if you raise your voice, and we're certainly not going to hit you or punish you."

Now you have accomplished the first step. You told the kids things are going to be different. But most important of all, you are going to have to demonstrate that to them. And you are going to demonstrate that by keeping calm and by allowing them to get angry at you.

At this point most of you are getting pretty panicky over a question that is bugging you. That question is, "If I let them talk back to me, what are they going to do next, openly defy me or beat up on me?" Absolutely not. You must draw the line and you draw the line with behavior. Your kid can tell you he is angry with you, but he cannot hit you. Or if you tell him to hang up his coat, he can tell you he does not like hanging up his coat, but he still has to hang it up. You draw the line with behavior.

You decided so far this business about expressing anger makes a lot of sense and you want to give it a try. You especially do not like the idea of your kids getting back at you indirectly, and you are willing to tolerate them giving you a problem once in a while. Good for you; that is a good start. Let us suppose you have even gone as far as to talk to mom about it and discuss it with the kids and tell them that you want them to come to you with their anger and tell you about it. Remember what I said earlier about change in families? Just because you have changed, does not mean the kids are going to change right away. If for ten years they have had to worry about getting a "knuckle sandwich" every time they talked back, they are not going to start expressing anger just because you say things have changed. They are not stupid. They are going to test the water by sticking a toe and then a foot in, before they jump in completely. That is okay, just be patient.

There are some other things you can do while they are getting up their courage. If you clash with one of the kids and he starts walking off into the other room and slamming his door, he is expressing anger by that action, but he is not expressing it directly or appropriately. Perhaps at this point, if you went into the room and said, "Hey, look. I just made you pretty angry right now. Wouldn't it be better if you told me about it instead of walking off and slamming the door?"

It is like priming a pump; you have to help him get started at pouring out some of the anger and the feelings. Keep in mind that it is going to be a slow process in change, but be patient and help your kid with the anger. You will both be a lot happier.

The first part of Rule 4 said, "Don't put up roadblocks to kids' feelings." All feelings tend to work this way, but particularly angry feelings. I have used anger because in our society it seems that it is one of the feelings we have the most trouble with. As a matter of fact, our expression or lack of expression of anger frequently sets the pace for other feelings. Children who have a great deal of difficulty expressing anger appropriately and directly, frequently do a pretty lousy job when it comes to expressing other feelings also, particularly love.

There is one last point I would like to make about anger. Frequently I am asked the question, "Is it bad for parents to fight in front of the kids?" The answer is not at all, providing you can do it in a reasonable way. It is important that, whoever is expressing anger, to do it *appropriately* and *directly* and *on target*. In other words, if you were mad at your boss, you would not come home and kick the dog, you would discuss it with your boss. Likewise, when parents are having hard feelings between themselves, it is perfectly okay, and in fact it is advisable, to fight it out in front of the kids as long as you can do it appropriately. It is fine to raise your voice and to say what you have to say, and then to kiss and make up. This is important for two reasons. As you will see in Rule 8, it is important to teach your kids by setting the example. You need to set an example for them of how to express their feelings and how to handle their anger and, in particular, how to control it. Certainly you would not want to hit your wife or use foul language or get carried away with your anger because you would be setting a bad example.

Secondly, it can be very reassuring to kids to see their parents fight and get over it. They learn that tempers can be controlled and people can really say what they have to say to each other and the roof does not fall in and the family does not split up. Frequently, when parents fight "not in front of the kids," the kids are very aware the fighting is going on either by hearing it or by seeing the expressions on parents' faces afterwards, but they do not really understand what the fight is about. All too often they will have daydreams or fantasies that are much worse than what has actually happened. In these daydreams they imagine that dad is going to kill mom, or mom is going to desert the family. Although it is not pleasant for anybody to watch a fight, as long as the fights are kept in reasonable limits and parents can make up afterwards, it is a good thing to do.

CHAPTER V

RULE 5: *Don't Make Kids Feel Like A Failure.*

There is one statement connected with this rule that is the most important thing to remember. That is, *a person who feels like a failure, acts like a failure.* It has been said that if you chip away at a kid throughout his growing-up years, when he gets to adulthood you will have a pile of rubble and debris. When you put kids down and you make them feel worthless, then they tend to act worthless.

I can probably best demonstrate this point by telling you about a fourteen-year-old boy named Jack that I saw last year. Jack was first referred to me from the school because there had been a sudden change in his personality, specifically he began getting into fights in and out of school, began lying and had recently been caught stealing from a local store. Both the school and the parents were quite concerned about this sudden change in Jack's behavior and sought my help for that reason. On interviewing Jack, I found a handsome, not terribly bright boy, who had a very nice personality. Talking with him did not add any clues as to the sudden change, so I spoke to the parents next. I asked them to tell me about any changes in Jack's life that took place about the time his delinquent behavior began. They recalled that just prior to the change in Jack, they had gotten so frustrated over his grades in school that they took him out of Little League baseball.

Then things started to fall into place for me in trying to understand the mystery. Let me summarize. Jack had always been of low normal intelligence or what we call "borderline." He was always a good boy who got along well with other kids, did well in sports and tried fairly hard in school. His grades were poor, but considering his intelligence, he seemed to be doing okay. His parents were unable to accept this. Over the years they constantly put him down and criticized him and chipped away at him for his poor grades. Every one of us, whether he be adult or kid, has to be successful at something, in order to be happy. I can feel pretty decent about myself because I go to work every day and try to help people. Or moms can feel pretty good because they take care of their families and cook and clean for them and make sure the children are raised right. It makes no difference what you do to feel good, just as long as you can do something, perhaps a little better than someone else, even if that is just building a pretty good birdhouse. What does this have to do with Jack? Jack was keeping his life in order and staying pretty straight because he was doing something that he felt was really worthwhile. He was a good athlete, and he was an outstanding Little League baseball player. His house was held up by just a few stilts; these stilts were his good looks, his getting along well with other kids and his doing well in sports. Jack obviously was not feeling successful as a student and, because of his limitations, probably never would make a career academically. But remember what I said, it is not that you "make it" like everybody else, it is that you can do at least one thing well.

After years of frustration Jack's parents unfortunately decided the nagging about his grades was not doing enough, so they took away the one thing that was really holding Jack's house up—Little League baseball—and sure enough, his house came crashing down. That is, he became delinquent.

Many parents try to get their kids interested in scouts, art, music, sports and an endless number of activities. Sometimes parents do this just to get the kid out of their hair, but I think the really important advantage in doing this with your kid is that you can help him find things in which he can excel. Suppose you try to get your daughter interested in ice skating, for example, and things just happen to click for her. That is great; you helped her find an area in which to excel, as well as an area in which she can feel good about herself.

While we are on the subject of activities, let me just answer a question that I am frequently asked, "Should I force my kid to go to scouts?" If you keep in mind what I said before about why you are trying to get him into new activities, I think the answer will be simple. Kids should not be forced into extracurricular activities. You are encouraging them to get involved so that they can enjoy it and, particularly, so they can find an area of success, something they can feel good about. If you force them to do something like go to scouts, they probably will end up hating it and will not be successful at all in that activity. In short, encourage, but do not demand extracurricular activities.

We have been talking about ways of building up your kid's self-esteem, his sense of worth. Let us look now at how not to tear him down. One way to do this is by using the approach, "I like you, but I don't like what you're doing." In other words, *condemn the act, not the kid.* As I mentioned before, it is fine to encourage your kids to be successful, but how about the everyday things they get involved in that are causing problems? We talked about things they do right, but how about all the things they do wrong? Whether we are adults or kids, we frequently do things wrong and whether we do them again depends on how we are handled.

Let us suppose that I had a boss who, day in and day out, criticized me and put me down. Even if he did this in a subtle way or by just a comment or a dirty look, after a while this would really get to me. The same boss then came to me after a year of this and said, "Say, Bob, I'm moving into a new house today. Would you please help me move the refrigerator and the stove in from the garage?" After a year of his bugging me I would probably tell him no directly or I would find some excuse as to why I could not help him. In other words, he would never get any cooperation out of me on or off the job if he put me down constantly.

The same thing is true of our kids. If we are constantly putting them down and criticizing them, they are not going to want to do anything to please us. And believe me, we need our kids' cooperation, particularly when we ask them not to get into trouble, shoot heroin or steal.

I am not suggesting for a minute that you cannot correct your kids, or tell them when they have done something wrong, but it seems to me the secret is in the telling, that is, in the way you tell them. For most of us, when we are angry, we tend to give a look of disgust or to say some things that we really do not mean. For example, you would be shocked to find out just how many parents regularly tell their kids they are stupid. Is it any wonder, the kids then flunk out of school? After all, they have been told for years that they are stupid and they are only doing what their parents have told them. Remember what I said earlier in this book about children living up to the parents' expectations.

I remember all too well a tragic case I saw a couple of years ago. This was a fourteen-year-old girl who came to me complaining bitterly that her mother always nagged her and put her down, and particularly how her mother always called her a "whore." I asked the girl if this was justified and if, indeed, she had been acting like a "whore." She said this had not been the case and when I talked to her parents they confirmed that. Further, mom admitted that it was her problem in getting very angry and saying things she did not mean. About a year later I saw this family again when the girl was pregnant. After years of her mom calling her daughter a "whore," she started acting like one.

I am asking you as parents to think before you speak. That is tough for all of us, particularly when we are mad, but it is something that you must do. "I like you, but I don't like what you're doing," is an ideal way to put it. For example, when you catch little Billy drawing with his crayons on the wall, do not say, "you rotten little kid." If you do, he will probably grow up to be a rotten big kid. It is better to say something like, "You know, Billy, you're a pretty good kid, but I sure don't like your drawing on the walls." In other words, condemn the act, not the kid. Kids can stand somebody criticizing their behavior, but they will not tolerate somebody putting them down.

CHAPTER VI

RULE 6: *Set Outer Limits, Giving Kids As Much Freedom As Possible While Encouraging Them To Take Responsibility For Their Actions.*

When I am out lecturing, this rule is by far the toughest one for me to get across to my audiences. I think there are some very definite reasons for that. One reason certainly is that the subject of responsibility is pretty vague. One kid might be able to handle the responsibility of brushing his teeth at age four and another kid might not be able to do it until age six. Therefore, one important thing to remember about this rule and about encouraging responsibility is that it is going to have to be tailor-made to fit your kid. No two kids are alike and therefore no two kids will be ready for the same responsibilities at the same time. However, when we talk about the various responsibilities I will try to give you a rough age at which I think you might try giving your kid that responsibility, but keep in mind you must be flexible about this. It is not important that the kid learns to pick out his own clothes at age eleven as opposed to age fifteen; what is important is that, *at some time* in his growing up years, his parents must stop doing it for him and insist that he do it for himself. Some of the most tragic situations I see in my everyday practice are when parents continue for so many years doing things for their kids that the kids should be doing for themselves; that is, some parents rob their kids of the chance to grow up by experience.

Kids have the right to be wrong. Kids will have to try certain things on their own, and they will have to learn the hard way that they do not work. Then they will have to try a new way. As parents, particularly when we love our kids a great deal, we try so hard to protect them from life. We try to teach them everything and hope they can learn by our mistakes, but unfortunately, that frequently does not work. Sometimes we can guide them, tell them, lecture them and punish them, but they will still have to do it wrong once or twice themselves to learn.

Let us start out with this concept of responsibility. When I think of the word responsibility I think of the kid being totally in charge of an 'area of his life; if he handles it well things will go well for him, and if he goofs up, he will have to suffer the consequences. Nowhere in this definition of responsibility do I mention a parent. You must keep in mind that there is only one captain on every ship. By this I mean only one person can be responsible for something in the kid's life. Parents and kids cannot be responsible for the same thing. If you are in a habit of laying out clothes each morning for your four-year-old to put on, you are responsible for picking out his clothes. That is not so bad until you realize that by your doing it, you are robbing him of the chance of making decisions, that is, of the chance of being responsible for something in his life.

I hear from parents of teenagers that their kids are not responsible. When I talk to these parents and question them carefully about how they raised their kids over the years, I find they never have given them responsibility for anything. If you want to be a good tennis player, there is only one way to do that. You buy a racket and some balls and you find a partner and you go out and hit the ball back and forth across the net every day until you get good at it. Sure, a little bit of coaching along the side (and I mean very little) might not be a bad idea, but for the most part, to be a good tennis player you have to practice a lot. That is the way it is with responsibility. To be a responsible person you have to practice a lot. You have to be given a lot of responsibility and practice it over a long period of time.

A responsible person for the most part is one who makes good decisions about his life. For example, if your fifteen-year-old kid walks into the woods one day and another kid walks up to him and offers him a "joint" (a marijuana cigarette), your son has to make a decision. Here again, if he has had a chance to make a lot of decisions throughout his lifetime, from the time he was very small on, there is a much better chance that he is going to make a correct decision and refuse that cigarette. However, if somebody has always done the thinking for him, he will not be in the habit of thinking for himself, and he will be less likely to make a good decision.

Let me use another analogy with you. Suppose I would like to build up my biceps (let us assume for the time being that becoming physically strong is like getting strong emotionally). There is one sure way to do that. I will get a set of barbells, and I will lift those barbells up and down, up and down, every day for about an hour. There is no doubt about it; I am going to build up my muscles and I will be strong. But suppose one day, as I am lifting the weights, you, my parents, are standing there watching me and feeling sorry for me because of all the hard work I am doing. Also suppose at that point I complain and say, "Oh, Mom and Dad, these are so heavy. Won't you please give me a hand with them?" The two of you start helping me lift the barbells up and down, up and down. That may be fine for you, but it is not going to be doing me nearly as much good as if I did it entirely on my own. Now suppose we go one step further and you say, "Gee, Son, let's help you even more." And you and mom continue lifting the barbells up and down as I recline on my chair and say things like, "Go on Mom and Dad, you're doing just fine." Again that is going to help you even more, but it is not going to be helping me at all.

This is exactly how it is with responsibility. As long as I am doing something entirely on my own it is going to be very good for me. If my parents start helping me with the responsibility or trying to share it with me, or worst of all, taking the responsibility completely, it is not going to help me at all.

As parents we take away responsibility sometimes faster than we give it. Let us suppose I give my kid an allowance when she is five years of age. Certainly, for the first or second week she is going to take that money and blow the whole thing on candy. Many parents at that point would say to their kid that she had blown the money so, therefore, she is not going to get any more. In other words, they would take away the responsibility. I think when a kid goofs up on a responsibility they need more responsibility, not less, so you should not take it away from them.

As a matter of fact, a similar situation did happen with my youngest daughter over her allowance. I started out when she was five years old by giving her a weekly allowance, out of which she was to pay for shows and popcorn (she liked to go to the show on Saturday afternoons). One week, shortly after we started this, she spent all her money on candy about the middle of the week. On Saturday, when it came time for her to go to the show, she said she needed some more money for the show. Of course, I replied that I was sorry, but money does not grow on trees and she would have to wait until her next payday. She shed a few tears over it but, most important of all, she learned the hard way that she has to be responsible for her money. Of course I continued giving her an allowance, and she learned the lesson that, if she wants to have money for certain things, she had better not spend it all. What is most important about this is that I did not take away the responsibility.

There are times that you will need to take away responsibility, but I encouraged you to do it briefly. For example, you have told your eight-year-old that he is only allowed to ride his bicycle in your neighborhood and you have walked very carefully around the neighborhood with him to show him exactly where you mean. Two weeks later you catch him riding his bike fifteen blocks away, in a traffic jam. I think at this point it is fine to take away the responsibility briefly. Perhaps you can tell him that he has gone farther than he was allowed to go, and for that reason, he will not be allowed to have his bike for the next two weeks. At the end of two weeks you give him back his bike and remind him why he had lost it, and off he goes again. As long as his bike is locked in the basement, he will never learn responsibility for it. Again, the point is, you only learn responsibility by doing.

That term "outer limits" is a term that some parents taught me and I think it is an excellent one. By this I mean, it is important for you to carefully define to your kid what he is allowed to do and what he is not allowed to do. The point I am trying to make is that, when you are doing this, err on the side of giving him too much freedom instead of too little. If you are not sure whether he can handle a bike for a three block radius or a six block radius, it is better to give him a little bit more freedom, the six block limit. You do this for two reasons; (1) so he can have more responsibility and get better at handling responsibility, and (2) the broader the rules are, the less likely he is to break them. Imagine drawing a circle on the floor with chalk and telling your kid to stay within the circle. If it is a small circle he is going to be tripping over the line constantly and getting into trouble with you for it. Whereas, if the circle is a large one, he will have a lot more freedom and end up not breaking the rules as often. Therefore, the two of you will get along better.

Let us talk more specifically now about responsibilities. There is one rough guideline that I would like to mention to you at this point, and I hope you remember it. You can teach kids until the age of twelve and after that, as parents, you just have to sit back and pray a lot. There is one area of psychology that I think everybody in the field would agree with, and that is when kids learn the concept of right and wrong. Some psychiatrists might say they learn it before the age of four, others would say six and others would say eight. But all of us, I believe, are in complete agreement that it is learned at a very early age. Certainly after the kid is into his teenage years, it is extremely difficult, if not practically impossible, to change his sense of right and wrong (his conscience). Yet isn't it sad how often parents of teenagers go on harping at them about the way they dress and the way they cut their hair, their friends and so many things in their lives, when there is no evidence in the world that this does any good. In fact, there is plenty of evidence that it does a lot of harm, because it just creates a lot of hard feelings and a lot of rebellion. So again, let me say that my philosophy on raising kids is to teach them until age twelve, to pray for them from twelve to eighteen and at age eighteen, to say good-bye.

Let me show you in a diagram what I mean by teaching kids responsibility.

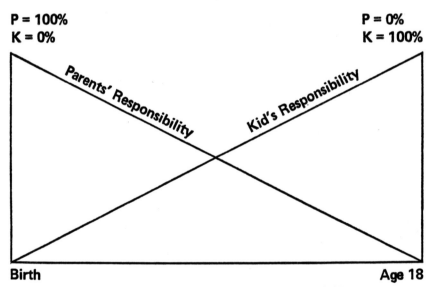

Figure 5. Parents' responsibility vs. kid's responsibility.

In the diagram above P stands for parents and K stands for kids. As you can see on the left, parents are a hundred percent responsible for a child at birth. If it were not for the parents feeding him, keeping him warm and taking care of him, the kid would die. And essentially, the kid is 0 percent responsible for his life. As you can see, parents' responsibility should *gradually* decrease until about the age of eighteen at which time parents should have 0 percent responsibility and the kid should be 100 percent responsible for himself. Keep in mind that this figure of age eighteen is a rough one and it is going to differ from one kid to another.

But what is important is that parents should gradually take less responsibility for their kid, and the kid should gradually take more responsibility for himself.

One child might be ready to get married and leave home by the age of seventeen, and another might need his parents involved, perhaps only financially, till he has finished college at age twenty one. But let us just use eighteen as an average figure for the child to separate from the family, either because of marriage, or going off to the Army or off to college.

While working at the University of Michigan I regularly saw some tragic things happening with a lot of teenagers. Their parents would take far too much responsibility for them for many, many years, and then suddenly would throw complete responsibility on them at age eighteen, when they went off to college. Because the kids had never had much responsibility before, they did not know how to handle it. Consequently, I would see them walking down the street in the dead of winter without shoes and, when I asked them why they were barefoot, they said they had mishandled all their money and there was not enough money left for shoes. These families might be diagramed like this:

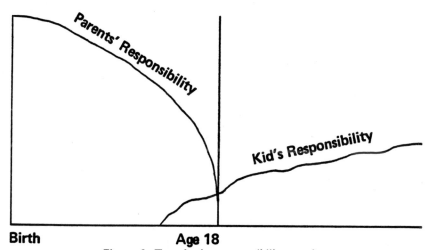

Figure 6. Transferring responsibility too late.

In the diagram above, you can see how some parents do it, and not very successfully I might add. They take way too much responsibility for their kids and then they try to stop suddenly when the kid leaves home. It is almost as if they wake up one morning and find their kid is eighteen instead of eight and get panicky and give him all the responsibility at once. I very frequently see parents who are still telling their kid what to wear at age sixteen. When I get them to stop and think about it, they feel pretty silly still dressing their sixteen-year-old.

That is an important point. Most of these things in the area of responsibility you will tend to do wrong unless you really think about them. My wife and I sit down every couple of months and talk about what new and added responsibilities we can give our kids. Perhaps they need a little bit more allowance, perhaps there are some added chores they can be responsible for, perhaps there are some new freedoms we feel they can handle. If you do not stop and think about these things, you will suddenly find one morning that your baby is grown up. And he has never learned to take responsibility because you have not given it to him all along, in gradually increasing doses.

Let us talk about some specific responsibilities and some ages that kids can start assuming these responsibilities, keeping in mind that this is going to vary slightly for different kids. By age two the kid should be responsible to pick out what kind of food he wants to eat, and also about that time you can start him on the way to being potty trained. He should start being responsible for what food he wants to eat, and when and where he is going to go to the bathroom. I cannot say it too many times; once you give him the responsibility for something you must no longer say anything about it. If you say, "What you eat is up to you, kid," then you should have nothing further to say about it. At age two to three he can be responsible for playing in or outside the house, and you should define the play areas both in and outside the house very carefully. About age four is a good time to start having the kid be responsible for brushing his teeth. Until that time you have reminded him daily and, if he has not learned by now, he is never going to learn. You tell him that, from now on, with his teeth he is on his own and hope for the best. Nagging him further will not help. By age five most kids can start picking out what clothes they are going to wear that day. Let me remind you that they may have to learn some things about this the hard way. For example, for a couple of years you have told your little girl that in cold weather you wear warmer clothes, but she probably will not listen to that. She may have to go out in the dead of winter in a little summer dress and catch a bad cold for it to really sink in.

I think age five is a good time to start sex education and I will talk more about this specifically in a later chapter. Also at age five parents can start giving their kids an allowance. It is always a good idea to frequently take a look at the kid's need for an allowance and, whatever you decide to give him, tell him exactly what you *expect* should come out of that. But then once you give a kid an allowance I do not think it is a good idea to tell him how to spend it. Do not say you have got to save half of it, or you cannot buy candy with it, or things like that. You should say, "Okay, Chuckie, you are seven-years-old now, and we are increasing your allowance to one dollar a week. Out of that dollar we expect you to pay for any shows, candy, entertainment or school supplies." You should try to make this very clear at first so he does not come to you later and say that he spent it all and now needs some more money for school supplies. If he does do that, then you can borrow my well-worn phrase, "That's life."

The trick is to take any given topic, like clothing, and figure out where the kids should be with respect to responsibility for clothing at any point in his life. For example, he can pick out the clothes he is going to wear each day at age five. By age eight or ten he should be going with mom to help pick out the clothes from the store. By age twelve or fourteen he should be going completely by himself to pick out his clothes and by that time his allowance should include enough money to cover the cost of clothing. At age fourteen, if he wants to wear ragged jeans and spend all that clothing allowance for records, I do not think you should stop him. You can tell him you are not happy about that, but, as I have said repeatedly, kids have the right to be wrong. The worst thing that will happen if you do that is that one day his friends will get on him about his ragged clothes, and he will have learned the hard way to improve his appearance.

As you recall from Rule I, however, there will always be some responsibility that you will have to take care of as long as the kid is living in your home. Remember, I mentioned particularly three areas; obeying the law, your knowing his whereabouts and his being in on time.

At this point, frequently parents get pretty upset with me again because I start sounding like a permissive psychiatrist, or else they misinterpret what I am saying and think that I am telling them not to care about their kids. Again, nothing could be farther from the truth. What I am saying is that responsibility only comes with a lot of practice. If you want your kid to grow up to be a responsible adult, you must start very early and gradually give him increasing doses of responsibility so he will get used to handling it and get in the habit of making good decisions about his life.

CHAPTER VII

Rule 7: *Try To Figure Out What The Behavior Is Doing For The Kid.*

As you recall in Rule 3, I said behavior that works, continues, and behavior that does not work is given up. Very frequently, if we can sit down and figure out what is behind certain behavior, that will give us some pretty important clues as to how to deal with it. Earlier I said to drop the word "why" from your vocabulary. I did not mean you should not think about why or should not ask yourself or your spouse why, but do not ask the kid why, because he rarely will know.

Are you ready to start thinking about some of the whys? Let us take some easy situations for a starter. Your two-year-old reaches up on top of the television to get some candy from the candy dish. You have warned him about that many times, so you walk over and in a loud voice you say, "No," and give his hand a firm smack. He screams, throws himself on the floor, bangs his head and his fists and kicks his feet. What is he saying by his behavior? Kids tell us things by their behavior and not by words, and it is up to us to figure out what they mean by it. This little two-year-old is probably saying a couple of things by his behavior. One, is that I am mad at you for not giving me a candy and I am going to show you how mad I am by banging my fists and kicking my feet. The second thing he is doing is trying to get attention; he did not get his first choice of candy, but he sure would settle for some nice love and attention of some kind in its place. When we analyze this kid's behavior he is showing his anger and he is asking for attention. This helps us figure out what we should do next. In this case it is pretty simple. The only thing to do is to ignore it and that way you will be sure you are not rewarding him by giving him attention (Rule 3) and you will be tolerating his anger (Rule 4).

Now that you have the hang of it, let us move on to some tougher behavior to work on. Let us suppose you have been pretty annoyed with your five-year-old daughter's behavior at the table. You have told her a couple of times you do not like her behavior and you tell her that if she cannot stop playing with her food, she will have to leave the table. Now it is her move. She sticks the spoon in the mashed potatoes and pulls back the top of the spoon and lets fly a big glob, striking dad squarely in the forehead. Now it is your move, but wait a second. Stop and think (I know it is tough when you are fuming like you are), and try to figure out what is behind the behavior. First of all, she is saying this is what I think of your rules, "thwack." The first meaning in the behavior is defiance (which is just another form of anger), but her expressing her anger by throwing things must be stopped. The second part of the message in her behavior is one of testing you to see if you are really going to follow through with what you said, that is, are you really going to send her to her room. Obviously here the answer again is simple. You do not want to show her that she "got to you," so you keep your cool and send her to her room and tell her that since she was throwing her food, she will have to skip the rest of the meal and spend that time in her room.

There are thousands of games kids play with their parents, and they actually can be humorous to look at, particularly if you are not the parent with whom the kid is playing. For example, there are two very common messages in kids wetting the bed and both of these are sort of a play on words. Let us take a six-year-old boy who is wetting the bed almost every night, and his parents unfortunately are scolding him and spanking him for it. Unquestionably, he is going to continue wetting the bed as long as they continue acting that way. The messages in his bed-wetting are (1) "Piss on you," and (2) "You're scaring the piss out of me." The first meaning is one of anger and resentment for the parents bugging him about it and punishing him, and the second message is one of fear of being spanked. The same thing can be said about kids who soil their pants. Further there is another reason why kids mess their pants and that is because parents who tear away at their kid's self-esteem and make him feel worthless will frequently have a kid who messes himself.

Once you think about the reasons behind the behavior you frequently can get some pretty good clues as to what to do about it. As you will see later on in the chapter on wetting and soiling, you can avoid these problems by ignoring the behavior and therefore not making the kid angry, fearful or making him feel worthless.

Also keep in mind again some of the things I mentioned in Rule 3 about how kids sort of accidentally stumble on new and delightfully different ways to get our attention. Examples of these things are stuttering, facial tics, pulling their hair out, poking at baby brother, etc. And, as you remember, attention-getting behavior must be ignored.

To further demonstrate this point about trying to figure out kids' behavior, let me tell you about a case I saw not too long ago. This was an interesting couple who came to me because their days started off so badly with their two children (age six and five), that everybody in the family was miserable. This problem had been going on for many months. It seems the father had to be at work by six o'clock in the morning. To do this he got up at 4:30 a.m., had breakfast and set out for about a half hour drive to his place of employment. Mother frequently would get up with him to fix him his breakfast and then would want to go back to sleep, or on other days would sleep in. The problem was that the children wanted in on it. Each morning the kids would get up when they heard dad's alarm at 4:30 and would insist on coming out and having breakfast with dad and "joining the family." Mother and father, however, were very upset by this for several reasons. They felt that was one of the few times they had to themselves during the day. Also, mother wanted to go back to sleep after dad left for work, but was unable to do so with the kids up and running around the house. For months they had had a running battle over this, with the kids crying about wanting to come out, and mother and father demanding that they stay in their rooms and go back to sleep.

After hearing about this upsetting family situation I suggested to the parents that we try and take a look at what was behind the problem. In other words, why did the children carry on so in the morning, upsetting the whole family? As we looked at it in the light of day, the answer was quite obvious. The children just wanted to be with their family; that is, they wanted to be *accepted* by their parents. But what they had been receiving over the last number of months, in their eyes, was total rejection. They did not understand about mom's wanting to go back to sleep, or their mom and dad's wanting some quiet to themselves. The only message they got out of the daily upsetting event was, "Mom and Dad don't love us and don't care about us, and therefore, don't want us around." Of course, they did not say that, but we can certainly make an educated guess that that is what they were thinking and feeling. Once we figured out what was behind their carrying on in the morning, the solution came easily.

At that point I suggested to the parents that instead of pushing the kids away so much, they start inviting them to join the family, even though it was 4:30 in the morning. Mom and dad agreed to give it a try. We all felt that, probably, if the kids did not feel like they were being pushed out, they would have no need to carry on so. That night, as we had agreed, mom and dad talked to the kids and told them that, from now on, they would like to have them join the family at breakfast and that mom would wake them.

The next morning mom did wake them as promised, and invited them to the breakfast table. They both sat there throughout breakfast looking quite sleepy but managed to get through a bowl of cereal. At the end of breakfast both children asked if they had to get up each morning, and when mom replied it would be up to them, they decided that they would rather sleep in. And in fact the problem disappeared permanently.

As is true in so many situations with kids, if they feel they are allowed to do something, then they frequently do not need to do it. By our figuring out what the behavior was doing for the kids, we were able to find a simple solution.

CHAPTER VIII

RULE 8: *Teach Your Kids In Two Ways, By Telling Them and By Showing Them By Example.*

It is no accident that I saved this rule for last. I am sure you and I are in complete agreement about the first part of this rule, that is, telling your kids what is good for them, and bad for them, and what is right and what is wrong. The bitter pill most parents have trouble swallowing is facing the second part of the rule, the fact that kids learn most of what they know by watching their parents, not by listening to them. Most of us as parents do not like to think about that, let alone accept it as being a fact. It is much more comfortable for us to think we can raise our kids, irrespective of how we behave, and they will grow up "right," because we have told them how to do it. If we can let ourselves believe that fantasy, then we do not have to look at our own behavior. Let us face it, looking at how we act is painful. Whether you are lying on an analyst's couch looking at your own actions, having a dispute with your husband or thinking about raising your kids, looking at your own behavior in any of these situations is not a pleasant thing to do and most of us tend to avoid it.

But when we pull our ostrich head out of the sand, the cold, cruel world is still staring us in the face. The reality is still there. Our kids are going to learn by watching us. Probably the most important reason we do not like to face this fact is that if we do face it squarely and honestly, then we have to change our actions. It is like the alcoholic who for years and years tells himself that he is not really an alcoholic, but that he is just a social drinker and tends to go overboard once in a while. As long as he tells himself that, he does not have to do anything about his drinking. Once he faces the fact that he is an alcoholic, then he cannot stand to live with himself unless he works on changing his behavior. So it is with us as parents. We kid ourselves into thinking our own actions are just, or acceptable, rather than admitting to ourselves that our own behavior is bad. Once we admit it then we must start to work on changing it and that is something very difficult for any of us to do.

Picture for a minute that your boss rides you day in and day out about your being lazy and your not working hard enough. But let us suppose further, that your boss is one of the laziest guys you had ever seen. He just sits around all day reading the newspaper and does not do any productive work. I would guess that it would not be very long before you would either punch him in the mouth or quit the job, or both. None of us likes to be criticized by somebody else, but the hardest thing to take is being criticized by a hypocrite.

The same thing is true for our kids. It is hard enough for them when we tell them what to do, but it is intolerable when we tell them what to do and cannot do it ourselves.

Let me give you some specific examples. I have seen a wide variety of hypocrites in my office, and I tend to divide them into two categories. First, there is the overt or obvious hypocrite. The second type is the covert or subtle hypocrite.

Let us discuss the overt hypocrite first. This is the guy that comes into my office, and I have to control myself to keep from laughing in his face. He sits there, lights up a cigarette and takes a deep drag that looks like it is going down to his toes. While he is exhaling, he begins shouting, "I can't stand my kid's smoking!" Now remember, we teach our kids what is "okay" by what we do. In other words, this father is giving his son two exactly opposite messages at the same time. On the one hand, he is telling him it is not good to smoke, and on the other hand, he is showing him by example that it is just fine to smoke. This kid has two problems now; one, he is furious at his hypocritical father and, two, he is confused, that is, he really does not know which message to respond to.

I am sure you all could help me add to this long list of overt hypocritical acts through your own observations. For example, the father who is speeding down the road in his car and lecturing his son on his careless driving, or the father who is standing there beating on his kid's backside and at the same telling him it is wrong to hit.

These are pretty obvious and hopefully we catch ourselves and try to avoid these more obvious kinds of hypocrisy. But I think even much worse and more dangerous are the covert or subtle ways in which we teach our kids bad habits. I think they are more dangerous because we even fool ourselves in doing it and are not even aware of what we are doing. So many of us act badly, but keep ourselves from facing our bad actions by justifying them. For example, I interviewed some blacks during the summer of the 1967 riots in Detroit and I asked them if they did not think what they were doing was wrong: the burning, looting and killing. They said, "Hey, no man, look how they have been treating us for the last 400 years." You have all heard that old expression, "two wrongs don't make a right," and it certainly is true. Burning, looting and killing are wrong, and they are bad deeds, regardless of who, or why, or what has happened before. But in order for these people not to feel bad about their bad actions, they tried to justify them on the basis of something that somebody else did to them.

But we all do this, and we do it every day. We do it in such subtle ways that we do not even notice it ourselves. For example, the business man who takes home a typewriter or pencils from the office where he works. If he allowed himself to face it squarely, that he was stealing it, he probably would not let himself do it, or would feel so guilty that he would have to take it back. What does he do? He justifies it to himself, that is, he tells himself, "Gee, they are such a big, wealthy company they'll never miss it." Or perhaps he tells himself, "They don't really pay me what I'm worth anyhow, so let's consider this typewriter a little extra bonus."

No matter how this guy fools himself, he is still stealing. No matter how he cuts the cake, it is still going to end up the same; he is still a thief. Where do the kids come into all this? They see the typewriter, and they know where it came from. Even though father gives them all his rationalizations and justifications and excuses, those kids are smart. They are not going to buy all that. They are only going to walk away thinking one thing: "Dad steals, therefore it's all right to steal." To make matters worse, this father will come in to see me probably ten years from now, when his eighteen-year-old son gets arrested for armed robbery, and will say to me, "Gee, Doc, I just don't understand why the kid would do something like that; I've given him such a good home and such a good upbringing."

Just remember one thing, our kids observe our bad behavior and learn by it. They do not listen to our excuses for it. There are many, many examples in this covert category. For example, the businessman father who drinks a great deal, of course because he is just entertaining his clients. Or the housewife who sips her sherry or her martinis all afternoon because the kids make her nervous. This couple is taking a drug, namely alcohol, to alter their mood and perhaps to even alter their behavior. As if that were not bad enough, they jump all over their teenager because they catch him smoking marijuana. It is funny how understanding parents can be of their own use of drugs, but just let their teenager try and tell them why he is using a little "pot," and they suddenly become so righteous, they stop listening.

I see many patients in my office who are totally inadequate sexually. A wife, for example, is frigid and just gets nervous any time her husband approaches her. How did she get that way? Her parents did not teach her that sex was bad. But let us take a careful look at what they did teach her. In her family, when this gal was growing up, her parents never talked to her about sex. In fact, every time it even came up tangentially people cleared their throats and got a little red faced. But worst of all, nothing was ever mentioned about it; the subject was taboo. There was only one message this girl could possibly get from that, that sex is so dirty and so bad, that it cannot even be talked about. In short, when the gal grows up, she understandably feels down deep, that sex is dirty and bad, and who could enjoy something that is dirty and bad. Despite all the headshrinkers and well-wishing friends who tell her she should not feel bad about it, she is still going to feel like it is dirty and bad because that is the message that was ingrained in her very early in life.

What I am saying and what is so painful for all of us as parents to face is that *kids are usually taught their bad behavior*. The kid who gets into fights because his father spanks him a lot, the kid that tells lies who has been lied to all of his life, the kid who cheats on a test paper because he watched dad cheat on his income tax. We accidently teach these kids bad behavior, but what is the difference whether it is accidental or intentional, they are still learning bad behavior.

I do not think I need to go further at this point elaborating on the thousands of ways we teach our kids by bad examples. I think what would be most helpful would be for each of us to take a good, long, hard look at some of the bad examples we are setting, and try to correct them.

Rules for Raising Kids

Dr. Lesowitz

1. There are battles you can win and battles you can't win; never fight a battle you can't win (potty, eating, grades, friends).

2. Always follow through and be consistent; don't make a threat you can't keep.

3. Don't get involved with kid's behavior unless necessary; praise good behavior and ignore bad.

4. Don't put up road-blocks to kid's feelings, especially anger.

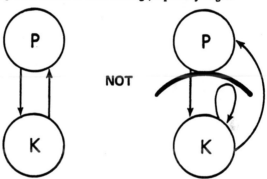

5. "I like you, but I don't like what you're doing." Don't make kids feel like a failure (condemn the act not the kid).

6. Set outer limits, giving kids as much freedom as possible while encouraging them to take responsibility for their actions.

7. Try to figure out what the behavior is doing for the kid.

8. Teach your kids in two ways, by telling them and by showing them by example.

PART II

SPECIAL PROBLEMS

I HAVE DEVOTED THIS NEXT PART OF THE BOOK TO SPECIAL PROB-
LEMS THAT FACE MANY PARENTS IN DEALING WITH THEIR KIDS.
NOW THAT YOU UNDERSTAND THE EIGHT BASIC RULES, YOU ARE WELL
ON YOUR WAY TO SOLVING THE MANY SPECIAL PROBLEMS THAT MAY
FACE YOUR FAMILY.

KEEP IN MIND THAT NO CHILD IS A PURE STRAIN; HE IS NOT JUST
A DISCIPLINE PROBLEM OR JUST A SHY KID OR JUST A BED-WETTER.
HE IS PROBABLY A COMBINATION OF MANY THINGS. I WOULD SUGGEST
READING ABOUT ALL THE SPECIAL PROBLEMS, EVEN IF THE CHAPTER
ON THE SURFACE DOES NOT SEEM TO APPLY TO YOUR CHILD.
YOUR READING THOSE CHAPTERS MIGHT HELP YOU PREVENT YOUR
CHILD FROM HAVING THOSE PROBLEMS.

CHAPTER IX

Discipline

By far, the questions most commonly asked of me concern discipline. The whole subject of discipline is something our society is really caught up in. If you ask somebody what comes to his mind when you say the word "crime," he will automatically respond "punishment." I have never heard anybody respond to the "crime" by saying "understand the crime," or "control the criminal." In other words, the concept of punishment is so automatic in our society, we do not consider anything else, when in fact, there should be a third step in this whole process. The three steps really are crime, stopping the crime and punishment for the crime.

Diagrammatically it looks like this:

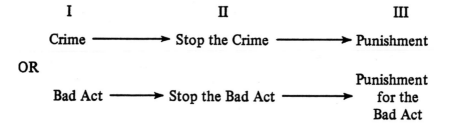

I	II	III
Crime ⟶	Stop the Crime ⟶	Punishment

OR

		Punishment
Bad Act ⟶	Stop the Bad Act ⟶	for the Bad Act

If we were to look at this sequence of events more specifically, we might use an example of a boy beating up on his sister, stopping the boy from beating up on his sister and spanking the boy for beating up on his sister.

At this point you are thinking what is so strange about that? That is just a beautiful example of how automatic a part punishment plays in our society. This may shock you, but there is little or no evidence that Step III, namely punishment, does anything to modify the kid's future behavior. Let me say that again. *There has never been any scientific evidence, whether psychological or behavioral, that adding that third step (punishment) helps at all* for the majority of kids.

Let us go back over the example of the boy hitting his sister. This young lad, let us say aged six, is standing in the living room pounding on his sister and she is crying. As a parent you want to break it up, but you also do not want this kind of behavior to continue in the

future. What do you do about it? I have already said that most of us
would automatically stop the boy from pounding on his sister and
then would punish him either by spanking or sending him to his room
or something like that. Yet there is no evidence that that last step
works. As a matter of fact, there is evidence suggesting that particularly with stubborn or predelinquent kids, punishment increases the
chance of it happening again.

What's the proper way to handle it? If you can just stick to Step I
and Step II, namely seeing the boy beating on his sister and stopping
him from doing that, your chances are going to be better of preventing it from happening again. When you stop him you can say, "Hey,
Paul, you don't hit your sister." Or if he refuses to stop, you control
him by holding him or putting him in his room, but that too in control, not punishment.

That is pretty hard for us to do. In fact, what I am really doing in
this part of the chapter is trying to make you aware of some things
that have been "born into us" as parents that do not make sense.
These things are so automatic that we do not even stop to question
them and I want you to stop and question them.

At this point it probably will be helpful to you to remember Rule
3: Don't get involved with kid's behavior unless necessary; reward
good behavior and ignore bad. Particularly, I want to remind you of
the concept that rewarding good behavior helps, but punishing bad
behavior not only does not help, but frequently make the behavior
worse because you have paid attention to it.

Why do we punish? We mainly punish because we want revenge.
The kids' fighting in the other room has upset us, we are angry, and
we want to get back at them (they have hurt us so we want to hurt
them). We punish by spanking or sending them to their room. But
after all, is that not a pretty silly reason for our doing something, just
because we want revenge? What I am really trying to get you to think
about is the difference between controlling behavior and punishing
behavior; controlling means stopping the action (even though it is
temporarily stopping the action) and punishing is for revenge.

I am not saying that revenge does not make us feel better, it sure
does. If my daughter does something wrong and I spank her, I am
going to be tremendously relieved of all that anger I was carrying
around. But all too often this is just a temporary relief for us because
it will not take very long until the guilt sets in, and then we feel

twice as bad because we have done something we are sorry for later. How do we adults change bad habits, like taking revenge?

Automatic behavior is defined as something we do without thinking about it. If we have some automatic behavior we are not happy with, the way to change it is for us to think about it. That is what I am asking you to do with this business of punishment. It is so automatic for us that we do it without thinking, and frequently with poor results. The next time your kid does something wrong, hopefully you will stop and think about it in terms of what is the act, and how can I stop the act without revenge or punishment. It is actually pretty easy to do, but to pull it off you have to think about it first.

Revenge is a terribly important word in raising kids and yet it is funny that very few authors talk about it. I think it is probably because they themselves do not like to admit that it is an important part of raising kids. You will see in further chapters on delinquency and other behavior that revenge plays an important part in why the kid is doing the things he is doing. Revenge plays an important part in what we do to the kid after he has misbehaved. After all, revenge is just the child in all of us. We need not be ashamed to admit that it is there or that we frequently want revenge, but what we need to do is to not let it happen.

I have often wondered why spanking works so beautifully with dogs and with infants (let us say up to two years of age). I think it probably has to do with this business of revenge. Let us say your dog snaps at you. You will probably say "No" in a loud tone of voice and smack him across the nose. This usually works very well and the next time the dog thinks about snapping, he associates snapping with the smack on the nose and he does not do it. The same is true of infants. If a one-year-old crawls up and reaches for the ashtray, you smack him on the hand and say "No" and he probably will not do it again. But dogs and infants are not sophisticated enough to want revenge. If you spank your eight-year-old, you are going to make him angry and he is going to think about all the ways he can get back at you (and he probably will).

Spanking is one thing that just about all parents of younger children ask me about, and I would like to devote this part of the chapter to the specific question of spanking.

First of all, I would like to make it clear that whether or not you spank your kid is entirely up to you. It is certainly your right as a parent to be able to spank your kid if you would like to, and in fact, it is your duty as a parent to think carefully on the question of spanking, and come up with a decision you feel comfortable with. It is important to make your decision in advance; by that I mean, if you try to decide whether or not to spank your kid while you are furious with him for breaking a favorite vase, your decision is much less likely to be a good one. Therefore it is much better to decide in a calm, rational mood whether you feel spanking is a reasonable punishment for your kid. Further, it is terribly important for both mom and dad to be in complete agreement as to whether they are going to use spanking as an approach to their kid's behavior. Some kids, as we all know, do not need to be spanked, while with others it may work. With still other kinds of kids it only makes their behavior worse. Certainly the more frequently it is used, the less value it has.

It is most important for you to decide if spanking will "work." Notice, I have been trying to stay away from terms like "right" and "wrong." This is not a moral question, and certainly if we look at it in moral terms, we will never reach a decision. However, I think it is more practical and more useful to look at the question of spanking in terms of, does it work or doesn't it? You have a decision to make about spanking. To help you with this decision I would like to offer you my thoughts and experiences on the topic of spanking, as well as what I think are the opinions of most people in the field. It will become obvious to you in a moment that I have a strong bias in favor of not spanking. Again, this is not because it is wrong or right, but because I feel it does not work.

Remember, in Rule 4 we talked about not putting up roadblocks to kids' feelings, especially anger. If you spank your kid, you are expressing your angry feelings toward him, but you make him too scared to express his angry feelings toward you. Kids are not stupid. They are not about to tell Dad they are angry with him while he is waving a belt over his head or swinging his fists. As you recall, either they keep it inside and have some problems result from that, or they try and take revenge in some roundabout way, such as doing poorly in school, taking drugs or getting pregnant, just to name a few. The first reason not to spank is that it almost always results in the kid keeping his angry feelings inside and not expressing them directly and appropriately.

Another reason for not spanking a kid is that, among other things, it creates a lot of anger. If you tell your kid to pick up his coat, he will probably pick it up and that is no big deal. But if you tell him to pick up his coat and smack him, you are going to make him mad. You have created anger in him that is completely unnecessary. And, as mentioned in the last paragraph, he is probably going to take revenge on you and get this anger out in one way or another. As you will see in the chapter on "lying and stealing," the best way in the world to insure that your kid continues to lie and steal is to keep spanking him. He will have to keep it up, even if it is just to get revenge on you.

By far the most common problem I see in kids is what the professionals call the oppositional or negative child, but what you and I would call the stubborn kid. To parents of a stubborn preschooler, his behavior is not that alarming. If they tell this little stubborn boy to pick up his toys and he does not (he does the opposite of what he is asked), it is no big deal. However, it is not that specific behavior that concerns us with the stubborn kid, but it is the *pattern* or the *habit* he is forming. In other words, if you tell a little kid to pick up his toys, and he does the opposite, it is no big deal. But if you tell him as a teenager not to shoot heroin and he does the opposite (because he has formed that habit), he is going to be in real trouble. You are probably asking at this point, "How did we get from spanking to shooting heroin?" I feel quite strongly that spanking just reinforces (encourages) stubborn behavior patterns in kids, which lead to more serious problems in their teenage years.

Another good reason to avoid spanking is that kids do not learn when they are scared. In most instances we spank our kids because we want to teach them something. For example, your little boy is playing with matches and you spank him. You have spanked him because you want to teach him not to play with fire, but there is a very good chance he will not even remember why you spanked him. You know how we all like to forget unpleasant things. Since the kid has gotten spanked while he was playing with matches, he probably will forget both the unpleasant spanking and the lesson you tried to teach him about matches. I would like you to picture that you are standing outside and a fifty-foot giant walks up to you, stands over you and growls and waves a club. Suppose further, just at that moment I walk up to you and I hand you a book and ask you to memorize a paragraph while this giant is standing over you feverishly waving his club.

Obviously you are going to be so worried for your life that you would not be able to give any thought to memorizing the paragraph. This is exactly what our children go through, because after all, when they are little, we are so much bigger than they are that we make them afraid for their lives. We know that we would not kill them, but they do not know that. They just do not remember when they are scared.

Very frequently we find ourselves spanking our children for behavior that should be ignored completely. Remember Rule 3? Frequently our kids do things to get our attention and by spanking them we have just rewarded their behavior rather than punished it because we have given them our attention. It is negative attention, but kids feel that negative attention is better than no attention at all. In most instances children's bad behavior is best ignored rather than punished in any way. To put it another way, ignoring our kids' bad behavior is the worst punishment of all.

When you spank a kid you are setting an example for him that I do not think you really want to set. You are essentially saying to him that when we get mad at people we hit them; that hitting is the way you want him to express his angry feelings when he grows up. I do not believe you really intend to teach him that violence is the answer to solving problems. You would probably rather teach him that it is better to talk it out.

Remember in Rule 8 that we talked about teaching by setting a good example and how we talked about accidentally teaching our kids to misbehave. Spanking is a beautiful example. Let me say again, that when you spank your kid you are teaching him by example to hit people when he is mad at them. We have some places for kids who grow up believing that; they are called jails. Kids who grow up thinking that the appropriate way to express anger is by hitting have all kinds of troubles throughout their lifetime, whether it be on the job, or with their wives, or with raising their own children.

If you went back over this last section of spanking and each time substitute "overreacting" for the word "spanking," you probably find something very interesting. That is, that spanking is just one form of overreaction and overreacting, no matter what form it takes, has many of the same effects. Whether you actually spank, threaten to spank or just holler a lot, you tend to make the kid fearful, shut off his anger and make him want to get revenge. It is not only the spanking you are going to have to work on but also all the special ways you overreact. *All overreacting is harmful.*

It is always very interesting to me that every time I suggest to parents that they stop spanking or overreacting they get angry with me. That has always been somewhat puzzling to me, but I think they get angry because they feel I am taking away their only weapons and I am leaving them helpless. But I am really not. There are so many other ways to stop bad behavior that work so much better than spanking and hollering. Let me mention some of these to you and then you make the decision as to what you want to do with your children.

As a group, these techniques are all lumped together under the heading of "isolation techniques." Remember, in Rule 3, I said you reward good behavior and you ignore bad behavior; when you no longer can ignore the bad behavior you put the kid in a place where you can ignore his bad behavior. In other words, you isolate him. There are three different kinds of isolation techniques.

The first kind of isolation technique is one we have already talked about, that is, ignoring the bad behavior. For example, with a child who is throwing a temper tantrum in the middle of the living room the best thing to do is for the entire family to actually pretend he is not there and to walk around him. This can be pretty grating on parents' nerves, and I find that sometimes mom's getting busy in the kitchen or dad's getting engrossed in a book can help them not react to what is going on. In essence, in this kind of situation what you are actually doing is isolating the kid without actually removing him, you are isolating him *emotionally* from the rest of the family. One of the added benefits of this technique, and I would certainly encourage this kind of isolation to be your first choice whenever possible, is that you do not ever accidentally reward his bad behavior by paying attention to it.

The second kind of isolation technique is to remove the kid from the situation. Remember when we were kids in school and misbehaved, the teacher would send us to the "cloakroom?" That has always been and still is one of the very best kinds of discipline and behavior control that you can use. Whether you call it a cloakroom or a quiet room or just have the kid sit on a chair in the corner of his bedroom, it is all the same and really works very well. In Chapter XVI, "The Teacher and Behavior," I will discuss in more detail the concept of the quiet room.

Let us suppose your seven-year-old Johnny is chasing his little sister around the house with a knitting needle. You should say to him, "Johnny, give me that knitting needle and go to your room and sit on your chair until you think you can come out and do not have to chase your sister with sharp objects." Now, some people would call that punishment. I would rather look at that as stopping the bad action and giving the kid a chance to think about what he has been doing wrong. By sitting calmly in the corner of his room (of course there are no toys within his reach), there is not much else to do but think about what he did wrong. There is a much better chance by using this kind of technique that the lesson you are trying to teach him is going to "sink in." If you will notice in that statement I made to Johnny, I added at the end that he should come back when he does not have to do "that" any longer. This keeps the kid from feeling rejected and does not give him the message that you do not love him or do not care about him. What you are indeed saying is that you want him there with you, but only when he can stop that bad behavior.

The third kind of isolation technique is isolating the kid from the offending object. Let us say you just bought Tommy his first two-wheel bike and you very carefully have shown him where he can ride it and where he cannot ride it. After about the second or third day, if that long, Tommy is going to be off down the road much past the limits you have set for him. At that point the ideal punishment is to isolate Tommy from the offending object, the bicycle. You would get him in the house and say to Tommy that he went farther than he was supposed to go and that for a period of one week he will not be allowed to ride his bike.

Another example of isolating your child from an offending object is the concept of "grounding." Suppose your daughter was supposed to be in the house by 10 P.M. and she strolled in at 11:30. She mishandled her privileges outside the home and she, therefore, needs to have them taken away for a while. "Grounding" means being confined to the house, with the exception of going out for school.

Frequently at this point when I am talking to parents, many of them will come back with pretty much the same statement, "But we've tried all that and it doesn't work!" When we talk further, however, we will usually agree that, if they have really tried it, they just have not tried it long enough or have tried it interspersed with a lot of hollering and hitting, which of course cuts down on the value of this kind of behavior control.

There are a few principles you should keep in mind in using isolation techniques if you really want them to be successful. First of all, if mom and one of the kids clash, then it should be mom who handles it. Most commonly we find that moms like to pass the buck and say, "Just you wait till your father comes home." Teachers frequently ask parents to take over, when the teachers should be handling the problem. *The person that has the problem with the kid should handle it,* whether that be mom, dad or teacher.

Another point is that when mom does handle it, she should always keep dad posted as to what is going on. If mom has grounded teen-aged Susie for a week and has not told dad about it, he is liable to come along in the middle of the week and take Susie some place with him, which completely undoes the value of the restriction.

Since we are talking about restriction, it is important to remember the limits should be set quite clearly. Suppose you say to Susie that she is confined for a week and she can get off of her restriction on Saturday. Does that mean Saturday morning, afternoon or evening? It would be much better to say Saturday morning at 8 o'clock. Frequently when kids break restrictions they use the excuse that they misunderstood when the restriction was to be over.

Another good technique is to give frequent reminders throughout the restriction. We grounded Tommy for riding past the limits on his new bike. Let us suppose Tommy's parents agreed the restriction would last one week. It is very important to tell Tommy at the time his bike is taken away the reason for that, as well as throughout the week to remind him a couple of times that he cannot use his bike because he went past the limits. Also at the end of a restriction it is a good idea to sit down briefly with the kid and go over what happened and why he lost his bike and what he is going to do about it next time. Repetition is an essential part of any education, in other words, the more you say it (up to a point) the better it is going to sink in.

It is also a good idea to start slow and work up when you are using isolation techniques. It is fine for the first offense to get a restriction or a confinement to the room, but that hopefully should be a brief one or, with Tommy and his bike, on his first offense he was restricted from his bike for a period of one week. The next time will cost him perhaps two weeks.

This discipline business is frustrating work for parents. But after all, you are not reading this book to find out the easiest way out of your responsibility as a parent. We all know the easy ways out; what we are seeking are the ways that work. These techniques work, but you must not get discouraged. There is a basic fact of kids—they need to test us. Even though we very clearly tell them what is going to happen if they do something naughty, they probably will have to do it anyway once or twice just to make sure we are actually going to follow through. An old professor of mine once told me that you sometimes have to do things with kids 4,000 times, but that does not mean the technique does not work; it just means that some kids are more stubborn than others.

I am frequently asked by parents what I think of religious training. You are probably wondering why I am mentioning religious training in a chapter on discipline. They do have a lot in common. We are talking about what many religious organizations talk about, that is, how do we improve people's behavior? I said earlier in this book and I repeat it again, kids behave well to please their parents. Our pleasure and our approval is what makes kids go straight. All the discipline in the world, whether it be punishment, spanking or isolation techniques play only a tiny role in motivating kids towards good behavior. Fear and guilt are not good ways to motivate people's behavior. In answer to the question of religion, I think religious training is fine, particularly if it soft-pedals fear and guilt. Tell your children to behave properly so their parents and other people will be pleased with them, rather than behave properly or you will be "damned and your soul will go to hell." Most people who were made to feel guilty as kids about bad behavior, behave badly anyway, but just continue to feel guilty about it. In other words, all the "guilt" and "scare" tactics did not change their behavior.

The last thing I would like to mention is the concept of "restitution." This is certainly a sound and accepted principle of discipline. The essence of this concept is encouraging (or even forcing if necessary) the child to make right his wrongdoing. When you discover your five-year-old drawing on the wall with his crayons, you should stop him, tell him you do not like his doing that and insist that he wash it off.

Let me summarize by saying that you should praise good behavior and ignore bad. If the behavior cannot be ignored, control it by using isolation techniques, rather than punishing out of revenge. Over-reacting, whether it be in the form of spanking, hollering or threatening, frequently does much more harm than good. Finally, encourage your children to make restitution for their wrongdoings.

CHAPTER X

Sex and Drug Education

I am devoting an entire chapter to sex and drug education because I feel it is terribly important. As I said in the introduction of this book, I have a very strong commitment to prevention of mental health problems and I feel a good sex and drug education program, both at home and in school, are essential for preventing problems in a kid's life. As we all know, however, education alone is not the answer. A kid must know more than just the facts about sex and drugs; he must be given some moral attitudes, that is, a sense of right and wrong about drugs and sex. What constantly amazes me is although it is well established that your child's sense of right and wrong is established before the age of seven, most parents leave the education of sex and drugs to when their child reaches his teenage years. Unfortunately, all the talking in the world is not going to embed your values into his conscience at that age. It is just too late. The facts about drugs and sex can be learned as the child goes along, obviously the older he gets the more he is capable of learning, but most important of all, the moral attitudes should be taught to your kids at a very early age, probably between the ages of three and seven.

As we all probably have seen ourselves, kids certainly get into trouble with drugs and sex even though they have been given all the facts and moral attitudes. It is not just the lack of information. One statistic that bears this out nicely is that approximately two thirds of all the abortions done in the United States over the last ten years were done on married women who should have "known better." In the next chapter, however, I will talk more about the other reasons for pregnancy in more detail.

In this chapter I am going to discuss in detail some guidelines to use in teaching your kids about sex and drugs. As you read over them, you will realize these principles are just as true whether you are teaching about sex and drugs or mathematics and history. That is one of the important points about teaching these subjects; teach them like everything else. The same principles that we will discuss are just as appropriate for teaching sex and drugs in school as at home.

The following are some principles for teaching your kids about sex and drugs:

1. *Educate yourself.* It is tragic, but so many parents "pass the buck" when it comes to teaching their kids about sex and drugs because they do not know much about it themselves. That is not bad in itself, but many parents get stopped at that point because they think it is a major undertaking for them to educate themselves. Nothing could be farther from the truth. There are so many people around in our society today who are quite willing to help you with the task that it is a shame not to take advantage of them. You might start out by going to the library and getting some books on the subject and doing some reading on your own. Having done this, your family doctor, the school nurse, planned parenthood organizations, just to name a few, are always readily available to help you. Also there are many places to send away for material that is either free or offered to you at very little cost. You could write to the American Medical Association, 535 North Dearborn Street, Chicago, Illinois, 60610, and ask them for some material. They put out very excellent pamphlets for various age groups on sex education as well as a great deal of material on drugs. Further you can write to the Children's Bureau, Department of Health, Education and Welfare, Washington, D. C., 20201, for other information on sex and drugs. Still further, the National Institute of Mental Health, Chevy Chase, Maryland, 20015, is an excellent place to write, particularly if you are interested in factual information on drug abuse. You see, there are many, many people and organizations who are willing to help you out in your task of educating yourself. As you can imagine, this is an essential first step in starting a good education program for your children. It is unwise and perhaps dangerous to teach your kids "old wives' tales." Often we hear teenagers say they do not trust their parents, or in fact, anyone over thirty years of age. Certainly one of the reasons they feel this way is that they have been fed so much misinformation over the years that they do not know what to believe.

2. *Overcome your own anxiety.* We were all raised with a lot of taboos about sex, and there is hardly one of us that does not get a little uncomfortable when our kids ask us some very direct or pointed questions about sex. Also, most of us are pretty uptight about drugs since we frequently hear about the terrible things that happen as a result of drug abuse. For these reasons it is understandable that most of

us are quite uncomfortable and anxious about these two topics. It is important, however, in teaching your kids about these subjects, to try to overcome some of your own anxiety. Certainly educating yourself first about the facts will help. Another way to overcome your tense feelings about these subjects is to discuss them frequently with other people. Talking it over with your spouse, your family doctor and other people will help a great deal.

Psychologically we are made up of two parts, our thoughts and our feelings. In many instances the thoughts match our feelings and that is as it should be. For example, if we are talking about a chair we can describe the chair, and our feelings are appropriate to the subject because there are not too many of us that get upset or tense over a chair. However, with topics like sex and drugs we have a certain amount of factual information making up our thoughts, but our feelings may be quite different and may convey completely different messages. For example, I might try to tell my daughter that sexual intercourse is a very normal way for adults to show love and affection, but if while I am telling her that, my face is red, I may be accidentally giving her another message, namely, that sex is bad. It is the "double-messages" that confuse and upset kids. It is best to straighten out your own feelings about these topics before attempting to educate your kids.

There are many institutions now in the United States that train teachers so they can do a better job in teaching sex and drugs. One of the ways to help these teachers overcome their feelings is for them to spend many hours in lectures and, in particular, in discussion groups talking about their feelings. Certainly, I am not saying every parent should be in group therapy before setting out to teach his kids, but you can accomplish many of the same things by discussing the topics with your spouse, your physician or other people.

3. *Start early*. As I mentioned before, a kid's sense of right and wrong is probably developed by the time he is about seven years old. Therefore, you can see that waiting till age nine or ten or even the teenage years is probably pretty late in the game to start trying to educate your kid. There is an old wives' tale that I would like to clear up right now. That is, that you tell your kids about sex "when they ask." It is the rare kid who asks all he needs to know at the right time. As a matter of fact, many kids, if you waited till they ask the right questions, might be into their fourth illegitimate pregnancy. Do not wait for that. I have found, in teaching sex and drug education classes in

schools, that many kids ask questions because they are already in trouble.

Another common misconception is that if you teach your kid too early, something bad will happen. Some parents feel teaching sex too early causes the kid to become perverted or preoccupied with sex. Nothing could be farther from the truth. As a matter of fact, the worst thing that happens if you try to teach your kid something too early is that it goes over his head. If you try to teach your three-year-old calculus, he will probably just get very bored, and it will go in one ear and out the other. The same is true of sex and drug education. Most children start getting interested in sex at an age that really surprises parents and frequently catches them off guard. For example, a little two-year-old boy is quite aware of there being some differences between himself and his baby sister when they are bathing. I remember very well one day when my oldest daughter was three, she came running into the house all excited and said, "Daddy, I just figured out the difference between boys and girls."

I said, "Oh, what is that?"

She replied, "Boys have one of these," as she held up her right index finger. It seemed the little neighbor boy had been standing outside on our picnic table trying to see how far he could pee. I was able to take advantage of that situation to discuss it a little bit further, and we were well into our first sex education discussion.

I think it is a good idea to take advantage of all the thousands of situations that come up. I have had the opportunity to talk with kids who have been raised in some very progressive schools where sex education was started in nursery school at the age of three or four. It was so delightful for me to talk to these kids who were now teenagers and who had unbelievably healthy attitudes towards sex without all of the taboos and anxieties we adults have. Hopefully you could give the same benefits to your kids.

4. *Use repetition.* As any well-trained school teacher can tell you, repetition is one of the keys to education. If you will recall, you did not have math or history just one time in grade school. You probably had very simple math in kindergarten and first grade and, as you went along, got it repeatedly in larger doses throughout the years. The same principles apply to sex and drug education. The dose is based on what the kid can understand. Perhaps you are wondering how to judge whether your kid is able to understand it. That is very simple.

Look at his face. If he is puzzled, you know you are going too fast.
It is important not to use the lecture method, but rather to discuss it
and ask him questions to see what he knows and to see what is sink-
ing in. As I said before, the worst thing that will happen is that it will
go over his head. If this seems to be happening, you can just slow
down or back off and wait a few months or a year and try it again.
Please keep in mind that kids can develop an uncomfortable attitude
at a very early age, particularly if their parents are uncomfortable
about the topic. Sometimes the way they show this uncomfortable attitude is by "playing dumb" and looking like they do not understand.
Try not to be misled by a blank look. Sometimes it means they do not
really understand and other times it means that they are just a little
uncomfortable, but you can usually decide that by asking them about
it.

What I am saying is that the "sitting down on the bed for the birds
and bees lecture" when your kid is nine is not such a hot idea. Repeated, gradually increasing doses of sex and drug education will work
out much better in the long run.

5. *Sex and drugs are best taught at home.* In our highly complex
society, all kinds of institutions have been devised to take over responsibilities that parents once had. Picture for a moment the log-cabin days
of Abraham Lincoln or the people who settled the West. They did not
have a truck coming by the house each morning to deliver bread, milk
and eggs, another delivery service to take care of the diapers and still
another to handle the family's laundry. It was the responsibility of the
parents to do almost everything, from teaching the kids about sex
and math to handling the religious training.

We have come a long way since those days and there probably is
not one of us who is qualified to teach our kids everything they need
to know. But that does not mean we should give up the responsibility
completely. We must share it with other institutions such as schools
and churches and community organizations. In interviewing parents
I find they frequently have one common misconception. "The school
will teach them about sex and drugs, so we don't have to." That is
not true. Many parents and organizations fight the school's trying to
give their kid a good sex and drug education. But even if they were
able to, they cannot do as good a job as you can. First of all, you have
the advantage of seeing your kid every day and particularly of catching
him when he is very young. As I have mentioned before, this is terri-

bly important. Also it is impossible for the school to teach moral attitudes. That should be a parent's right and responsibility; after all, moral attitudes are different in every family.

In short, schools, family doctors and other people can help out, but it is primarily your responsibility to teach your kids about drugs and sex and, particularly, to teach them the moral attitudes, the sense of right and wrong. As parents our moral attitudes differ greatly. We must teach our own values to our kids, not the values of the teacher or the pediatrician.

Some parents teach their kids that premarital intercourse, for example, is okay. That is their right and responsibility to teach that to their kids if that is what they believe. The comedian, Woody Allen, was once asked how he felt about premarital intercourse. He replied, "It's okay, if it doesn't delay the ceremony."

6. *Keep it in context; don't overdo it or underdo it.* Probably because of our own discomfort many of us miss golden opportunities to teach our kids about sex and drugs. Some of the best discussions I have had with my kids have been in the context of something that has been happening in their everyday lives. For example, one time following a TV story where one of the characters was smoking marijuana, I asked my kids what they thought about it. We were able to get into a very interesting discussion of not only marijuana but many other kinds of drugs. There were many other golden opportunities such as when some friends of ours were changing their little boy's diaper in front of my daughters. Or when you are with your kids and you see a pregnant lady walk by, try asking them what she has under her dress. In other words, there are thousands of everyday occurrences in kids' lives we can use to our advantage as the jumping off point to get into a discussion of sex and drugs.

Let me explain now what I meant by overdoing or underdoing. Let us suppose you have never talked to your kid about sex and suddenly you turn around and he is twelve years old. If at that point you sit down for a formal "birds and bees lecture," he is going to see it as something strange. Nothing else in his life was taught to him this way, and he is going to get the idea that something is different or even "spooky" about this topic. It is so much better to teach it as you go along, instead of in one big dose.

Speaking of "dose," there was a very interesting study done in postwar Germany with our occupying forces there. Commanders were very

upset about the tremendous amount of venereal disease they were seeing so they panicked and asked physicians to start giving very formal
lectures on venereal disease. Some years later it was noticed that following these lectures there would always be a tremendous rise in the
amount of venereal disease. It was later theorized that perhaps a GI
was sitting listening to the lecture, who had not thought much about
sex recently. These formal lectures complete with exciting pictures
served as a reminder to him how long it had been since he had "had
some." Following the lecture he probably jumped up and went out
and got a dose. This, I think, is a good example of some of the problems you get into when you overdo it, and particularly when you
overdo it in a very formal way.

7. *Clear up misconceptions.* Some years ago I had a very interesting experience while at the University of Michigan interviewing hundreds of pregnant girls who were requesting an abortion. Their ages
ranged from fourteen to forty-five. In trying to get a detailed history
I would always ask them how it was that they happened to get pregnant. I was astounded at all the misconceptions they had about pregnancy, and it seemed to me that these misconceptions contributed
greatly to their getting pregnant. For example, when I asked one fourteen-year-old how she happened to become pregnant she replied,
"It happened when we hit a bump on my boyfriend's Honda." I was
quite puzzled by this since it was a new trick that I had never heard
of. When I asked her to explain it more carefully she unravelled a very
strange misconception to me. It seems that she thought that the egg
was suspended very carefully some place in the abdomen and that
while riding along on her boyfriend's Honda, they hit a bump and
shook the egg loose. She thought that is how her pregnancy started.
It never occurred to her that having intercourse all those times had
anything to do with her pregnancy.

That may sound funny to you, but for a fourteen-year-old pregnant
girl, it is a real tragedy. So many of these misconceptions lead to preg-
nancies, venereal disease and, worst of all, severe sexual hang-ups in
later life. Some of the reading I mentioned earlier can help you clear
up many of these misconceptions with your kids. Reuben's book,
*Everything You Always Wanted to Know About Sex, But Were
Afraid to Ask,* is an excellent book for clearing up your own misconceptions.

8. *Be honest and open.* A few years ago I was in the locker room at

the gym changing clothes to play handball when I overheard a conversation between a father and his sixteen-year-old son. Apparently the father did not want his son to see the movie "Midnight Cowboy." In order to keep his kid from going to the movie he was lecturing to the kid about how the movie was "lewd, glorified homosexuality and encouraged perversion," and would not let the kid go because it was so "filthy." The movie, in fact, did none of those things. The point of all this is that someday his son is going to actually see that movie and think his father had lied to him. Further, he will probably think that "if he lied to me about that, he has probably lied to me about many other things; I just will not believe him any more."

The price we pay for being dishonest with our kids is that they will not believe most of what we tell them.

If we do not teach openly and honestly about sex, kids grow up thinking it is too dirty and too horrible to even talk about, and I am sure that is not an attitude you want to give to your kids. As a matter of fact, when we do not talk openly about sex and drugs, it makes kids want to learn about them even more. An interesting statistic is that a number of years ago, when pornography was legalized in Denmark, sales immediately went down forty percent. It is also interesting that since pornography has been legalized there, Denmark has the lowest incidence of sex offenses in the world.

9. *Let the kids participate.* All too often adults try to design education programs, whether in school or at home, based on what they think is reasonable or what they want the kids to know. But we are adults and they are kids and chances are that they are not particularly interested in many of the things that interest us, and it is pretty hard to second guess them. Therefore it is a good idea when you are teaching your kid at home about sex or drugs, or if you are a teacher designing a school program, to always ask the kids what they are interested in hearing about. Certainly, as I mentioned earlier, you would not want to teach them only the things they ask about, but they can help you give them a more well-rounded program of education. Also by doing this you can see just about how far along they are in their education.

There are several meanings to that word, "participate." It also means you should discuss the topic with the kid, and do not "talk at him." Casual informal discussions in small groups are probably the single most effective way of communicating thoughts and ideas and feelings. In particular with such sensitive topics as sex and drugs, a discussion of the kids' feelings as you go along is absolutely essential for doing a complete job of education, and certainly a lecture situation does not provide an outlet for feelings.

Last of all, "participate" means letting the kid teach other kids once he has acquired a thorough understanding of the material. You probably have all had the experience, while teaching someone else about a given subject, you learn even more about it yourself and get a better understanding of the material. I have observed some excellent school programs where sixth, seventh and eighth grade students have gone into classes of their own age or classes of younger kids and done an excellent job of teaching sex and drugs. Not only do the kids benefit themselves, but they have a rapport with other kids that helps greatly in the process of education. Many times kids will feel much more comfortable discussing a topic with other kids than with adults, be they parents or teachers. For any of you who were raised in a large family, you know first hand how much of the social education came from your older brothers and sisters rather than your parents and teachers.

I am not at all suggesting that this is a "way out" for you parents or teachers. Do not let yourself pass the responsibility for sex and drug education to other kids in the family or other kids in the school, but rather use them as a supplement to your own teaching.

10. *Do not scare, threaten or produce guilt.* No boy ever stopped masturbating because his father told him he would go blind or it would cause him to grow hair on his palms. Perhaps you have heard the story about the little boy whose mother caught him masturbating. She then proceeded to tell him that if he did not stop, he would go blind. He asked, "Gee, Mom, can't I just do it till I need glasses?"

Just ask any psychiatrist what makes up the majority of complaints of people who come to him. He will probably tell you that most of his patients have sexual hang-ups. That, probably in a large part, comes from their parents trying to scare them out of having sex or by trying to make them feel guilty about it. Most of us adults have many hang-ups about sex, but let us not pass them on to our kids. Believe it or not, our kids will make excellent decisions about drugs and sex based on logic. They do not need to be scared or made to feel guilty. If given some moral attitudes while they are young and provided with good factual information, they will probably make better decisions when it comes to sex and drugs than we ever did.

At this point I would like to share with you my feelings about teaching birth control. Many parents have the funny idea that, if their kids know about something, they are going to try it. They are afraid a book on sex education will be taken as an instruction manual on how to do it. This is certainly incorrect. When your kid sees in the paper that some joker killed himself by trying to fly off a ten-story building, he does not run out and try it. Of course not, he uses his own good judgment. Such is the case when he learns about intercourse; he will not run out and try it just because he heard about it. Although you may wonder about it sometimes, he probably does have pretty good judgment.

Teaching kids about sex without teaching birth control, is like teaching a kid to drive a car without showing him where the brakes are. To leave out such an important part of the whole picture is certainly unwise and perhaps even dangerous. Even though your religious or personal values dictate that you feel birth control is wrong, you can still teach him it exists and, of course, tell him you do not feel it should be practiced. Telling your kid that there is such a thing as homosexuality does not mean you think it is a good idea, but he still has the right to know it exists. As a matter of fact, he is going to find out about it anyway. Wouldn't it be better that he heard it from you correctly, than to hear an inaccurate version from the "gutter"?

The best way to teach your kids a healthy attitude towards sex and drugs is to educate yourself and then teach them in gradually increasing doses, starting when they are young. Be honest and open. If you teach them good values and give them good information, they will make excellent decisions.

CHAPTER XI

The No-No's: Smoking, Drinking, Sex and Drugs

I have put these four problem areas together in one chapter for a number of important reasons. First of all, if you ask many parents how they feel about long hair, some would tell you it bothers them and others would say it is no big deal. However, if you would ask many, many parents, as I have, how they feel about their kids' smoking, drinking, participating in sex and using drugs, particularly at an early age, almost all parents would agree that these are definitely problems.

Another feature that these four topics have in common is they are all preventable problems. I feel strongly that if you follow the eight basic Rules For Raising Kids as your children are growing up, these four areas in particular will not turn out to be problems. Let me clarify by saying that following the eight rules will not guarantee, for example, that your kid will never taste liquor. What I am saying is there is an excellent chance that he will never develop a drinking problem. I think most of us as parents would agree that that is really what we would ask of our kids. I hope, for example, that my daughters, even though they may some time in their young lives experiment with drugs, never develop a problem with them.

Another feature that the four no-no's have in common is that they frequently share the same underlying causes.

Finally, the solutions to problems of smoking, drinking, sex and drugs are similar.

Let us now take a look at some of the "whys" kids get involved in smoking, drinking, sex and drugs. Suppose a patient were to come to me as his family doctor, and he were to tell me that he has had a fever of 102 degrees off and on for about two weeks. I would be doing a terrible disservice to tell him to take two aspirins and call me in the morning. In other words, if I did not look into the "whys" for his fever, the underlying causes, there is a very good chance the aspirin would not help him, and he would become much worse. I would have to take a good long look at this patient, examine him and perhaps run some tests on him to find out what is causing his fever. It may be something simple, like the flu, that he would get over pretty much on his own with very little professional help. On the other hand, he might have something very serious like tuberculosis, which would need a great deal of attention.

It is the same with problems of children. It seems to me that the approach some parents take, "Oh, it's just a phase he's going through and he'll probably outgrow it," is unwise and perhaps even dangerous. It is important to look into the "whys" for kid's doing things. Probably a good understanding of the eight basic rules at the beginning of this book will help you in understanding some of the "whys." There are some more specific "whys" that kids get involved in smoking, drinking, sex and drugs that I would like to discuss here. Please keep in mind however, that many of these "whys" will differ for different children.

Take a look now at some of the reasons why kids get involved in the four no-no's:

1. *Curiosity*. Certainly curiosity is an important reason for kids at least experimenting with smoking, drinking, sex and drugs. Perhaps you recall in your childhood wondering what it would be like to take your first puff on a cigarette or your first drink. It is an intense curiosity that, for many of us, can only be satisfied by giving it a try. Sometimes that is not at all dangerous. In fact, I have encouraged my children to experiment in front of me if they feel they have to try it. For example my oldest daughter came to me a few years ago and said, "Daddy, I know you've told me that smoking is bad for people because it probably causes lung cancer and heart disease and a bunch of other bad things, but I sure wonder what it feels like to smoke."

It seemed to me to be a healthy kind of curiosity, so I lit a cigarette for her and told her how to inhale it, and let her have a try at it. Of course you know what happened. She took a deep drag on the cigarette, coughed and choked and ran into the bathroom to throw up. Her curiosity had been resolved by trying and she, since that time, has never tried it again. Kids have a right to be wrong. It is probably a pretty good idea to let them experiment in front of you with many things they are curious about, providing the experiment would not be dangerous to their mind or body. For example, I would never experiment myself, nor would I let one of my kids experiment with LSD. For in this case, the first try might be psychologically disastrous. I am reminded of a number of teenagers I have seen who have ended up in the state hospital for years following their first "experiment" with LSD.

2. *Poor teaching.* As you recall in Rule 8, I said that it is important to teach kids in two ways, by telling them and by showing them by example. In Chapter X I stressed the importance of giving your kids a good factual and moral education, particularly at an early age, about such things as smoking, drinking, sex and drugs. I further said that most kids, given good honest factual information, will usually make excellent decisions. But let us face it, many kids do not receive a good education about the no-no's. Frequently because of our own uncomfortable feelings on these subjects as well as our fears that our kids might try these things, we do not do an adequate job of teaching them about these subjects.

Also, as you will recall from Rule 8, I mentioned how often we as parents, whether knowingly or unknowingly, set a bad example for our kids in these areas. I talked about how many of us parents smoke, drink, and use various kinds of drugs (alcohol), and yet we somehow expect that our kids should not follow our example. Further, it is distressing to hear how so frequently in our society, promiscuity and extra-marital affairs are becoming almost commonplace for adults. Is it any wonder that so frequently our children develop some pretty unhealthy attitudes and behavior toward sex?

3. *Peer pressure.* In the Appendix I have included a chart which describes the essential differences between children, teenagers and adults. I stress under "source of values" that teenagers look to their peers (friends and kids their own age) for their sense of values. They decide what is right and wrong by what their friends do and tell them. For a teenager, peer pressure is extremely great. Even for the kid who has had an outstanding upbringing until that point, his teenage years offer a real threat to his actions because the peer pressure is so strong. If, particularly, in his earlier childhood a boy has not always felt accepted by his parents, he may seek acceptance from his peer through bad behavior. I would like to expand on this business of peer pressure.

When we were kids things were a lot different. The kid that was "accepted" by the peer group was the kid who was nice looking, had a nice personality, was bright and did well in school, or the kid who excelled in socially acceptable activities, like being the football captain or the high school cheerleader. In the last decade the pendulum has unfortunately swung to the other side. It is tragic, but it seems so often now that the kid who is most accepted by the peer group is the one who is the sloppiest, gets in the most trouble or even the one who uses the most drugs. I do not really believe the peer group really accepts these kids, but many teenagers think the way to be accepted is to "be the best hippy on my block." And, after all, it is what that teenager thinks, not what I think, that is going to motivate his behavior. I am convinced the pendulum will swing back to a healthier resting place in the next few years, but in the meantime we must keep in mind that our kid's wanting to be somebody can be a strong motivating factor for them to smoke, drink, get involved with sex and experiment with drugs. I have seen a few teenagers who have felt that it is better to be the biggest "dope-user" in the school than to be a "nobody."

4. *Excitement.* I am sure none of us are too old to remember that doing something was more fun and exciting if it was a no-no or if it was a little bit dangerous. If there were no danger involved, I am sure there would be no such thing as a Grand Prix or a LeMans. If it were not dangerous, who would shoot the Colorado rapids in a rubber raft, or climb Mount Everest? What kid would hide behind the barn to smoke if "it were legal" for him to smoke in the house or at school? You see that things being dangerous or making them no-no's sometimes adds to the excitement and to the need for our kids to try things.

5. *It feels good.* How many times I have tried to "talk some sense into" a sixteen-year-old girl who has been having intercourse for a number of years. It is pretty hard, if not impossible, for me to change her attitude about something that she knows, by experience, she enjoys. How would we as adults feel if someone asked us to give up sex? Despite all the logical reasons in the world someone might give us, we would still be pretty reluctant to stop doing something that feels good. Unquestionably, there is a lot of pleasure involved with smoking, drinking, sex and drugs and, let us face it, we all like to do things that feel good.

6. *To stop emotional pain.* This again is very much like the "ostrich principle." If they can stick their heads in the sand, get drunk or get stoned on hash—even though it is just temporary relief—for many kids it is worth it. There are many kinds of emotional pain that all of us face every day, but hopefully as adults we have learned more reasonable ways of dealing with it. A teenager whose parents are riding her constantly may seek relief by getting involved with drugs. This, in

particular, is an area where we parents frequently set a bad example. Whatever happened to the old idea of laying down on the sofa for a half an hour when you have a headache? That works pretty well, but most of us reach very quickly for the aspirin bottle to get "instant relief" for our pain. Is your headache really any different from the emotional pain the girl was feeling whose parents were "bugging her"? Or how about the father that has to unwind from a hard day at the office by having two or three martinis? He is setting an example of chemically changing his mood.

What it boils down to is that kids hurt all the time, emotionally. That is an essential part of growing up and becoming mature. We reach maturity by facing obstacles and overcoming them or by having problems and solving them. Picture in your mind for a moment that life is like a very long race. At regular intervals along this "steeple chase course" are hurdles. Every time we jump over a hurdle successfully, we are a little bit better prepared to face the next hurdle. And so it goes through life; each hurdle you jump makes you a little bit stronger.

Now let us suppose while you are running along this race, you go under or around one of these hurdles. In other words, you "cop out" or take the easy way out. That hurdle, then, is not going to do you any good because you have not faced it directly. So it is with all of us in the everyday little hurdles we face. If we meet them squarely, we get stronger and more mature. If we take the easy way out and avoid the problem, we do not grow to maturity. Some of the many ways kids and adults run away from problems are by getting involved with drugs and drinking and sex. These things give us a temporary relief from our emotional pain, but when the drug wears off, the high is gone or the orgasm is over, the problem is still staring us in the face.

7. *To get back at their parents.* Remember in Rule 4 I talked about kids using indirect ways of getting back at their parents, and how frequently these indirect ways are self destructive. I do not think I have ever seen a pregnant teenage girl who has been getting along well with her parents. Almost always there has been a situation in the family where the parents have been bugging her and where both sides do not talk to each other. Try, for a moment, to put yourself in the skin of a sixteen-year-old girl whose parents are "on her" all the time. You would want revenge, and to get revenge you would not think much about what is going to hurt you; you would only think about what is

going to hurt your parents and then do just that. I am not saying kids do this consciously or deliberately, but they do it just the same. What is the difference whether a girl gets pregnant for conscious or unconscious reasons? She is still pregnant. For so many of our teenagers we have put walls up that prevent them from letting us know how they feel and from ever getting angry at us directly. We have left them no other route other than the indirect route to get back at us. And they are going to get back at us "where we live," in areas we are very sensitive about, like smoking, drinking, sex and drugs.

Of the seven "whys" I have just discussed, I think by far, this last one on revenge is most important.

I promised you in the introduction to this book, that I would not get caught up in giving you a bunch of psychological platitudes about kids. But rather I said I would try to give you some specific guidelines to follow in dealing with problems. I would like to do just that with respect to smoking, drinking, sex and drugs.

Let us take smoking first. This is a three-step program: *educate them, set a good example and then leave the rest up to them.* Starting when my kids were three years old, I talked to them about the dangers of smoking. I tried to explain to them why some kids smoke and how smoking can probably result in lung cancer, heart disease, emphysema and many other problems.

Because I did not want to be a hypocrite, I quit smoking myself. There were other reasons I quit smoking; for example, I saw my health going downhill. My wife, on the other hand, was unable to quit smoking at that time, and my kids were the first to bring that up to me. When they would say to me, "But Mommy smokes," I would not try to justify it or say it was okay for her (of course it is not). I did, however, explain to my kids that sometimes habits once formed are very hard to break. As an example, I reminded one of my daughters how difficult it was for her to stop sucking her thumb when she was little. It would be extremely unwise for us as parents, to say smoking is all right for older people. It is just as bad for us, if not worse, as for our kids. Besides, kids see right through those statements and realize we are just feeding them a line. Then they stop trusting us.

The third part of this program, and probably the most important part, is to leave the decision up to the kids. This is certainly the most scary part of the whole business. Of course, I do not like kids to smoke because I know that it is unwise, harmful and dangerous. But I honestly believe, and have seen it work hundreds of times with my patients, kids will make much better decisions if we give them the facts, set a good example and then leave the rest to them. In concluding my talks with my own kids about smoking I have always added the statement, "But after all, they are your lungs and it's your body, so you make the decision as to what you want to do about it." Remember I said earlier, that kids have the right to be wrong. At some time in the future my kids may decide to start smoking, but the chances of that happening are much fewer if it is truly left up to them.

Those three steps I mentioned are just as appropriate when we talk about drinking. I was raised in a home where drinking was left up to me. Occasionally we would have a glass of wine during religious ceremonies or for other special occasions. The liquor cabinet was never locked or watched. In fact my parents would offer me a glass of wine or beer with a meal if they were having it, but that was quite rare. The whole subject of drinking was not handled like no-no, but as a fact of life. That is, some people do it, and I had the right to make my own decision about it. Further, my parents set an excellent example by drinking very rarely, and when they did have something to drink, it was done in moderation. I can say proudly that I drink very little. There were times in college when I would have a little bit too much to drink. But those times were only occasionally and drinking never got to be a problem for me. That is the whole point; if handled correctly, your kids will learn to use these things wisely. It is not that smoking is bad or drinking is bad or sex or drugs are bad. The point is they need to be used in moderation and used wisely.

I think the three-step approach of educating the kids, setting good examples for them and leaving the rest up to them is just as important and appropriate for preparing them for sex and drugs as well. If you do a good job, these areas will not develop into problems. I realize first hand how scary it is today to tell your daughter that it is her body and sex is up to her, but if you have done a good job as a parent, you will not be disappointed.

The topic of drugs is a little bit more difficult because of many drugs being illegal, and certainly we cannot give kids the message that it is up to them whether or not they break the law. Let me just share with you the approach I use when I am asked to talk to groups of kids about drug problems. I try to stay away from the approach that there are good drugs and bad drugs, for that really is not true. It is true that all drugs can be used wisely or unwisely depending on the person, the circumstances and the dose. It was discovered a few years ago that some kids in California were injecting peanut butter in their veins. Peanut butter itself is not a "bad drug," but like anything else, can be used unwisely. There are many good uses for the "illegal" drugs, for example, morphine used in the relief of pain following surgery.

When kids talk about marijuana being safer than alcohol, they probably are correct in many respects, particularly medically speaking. However, even with a fairly benign drug like marijuana, I think there are some important social dangers involved. For example, probably the worst thing about marijuana is that it is illegal. By this I mean that the marijuana may not hurt your kid's body or mind, but it sure will hurt him socially. The medical dangers of using marijuana are probably not bad, but getting placed in a juvenile home for drug abuse or getting something on your permanent FBI record for drug abuse will be very harmful to you later on in life. For example, you cannot get into a medical school if you have had a felony conviction, and you cannot become a member of The American Bar Association. So you see, even the most benign drugs have their dangers, either physically, mentally or socially.

Another concern I have about kids using drugs, regardless of what drug they use, is that frequently they change their circle of friends. As they experiment and then get more involved in drugs, they stop hanging around with the "nice, clean-cut kids" they used to associate with. They cannot very well hang around with these kids because they are doing something illegal now, and the straight kids do not want to have anything to do with them (and vice versa). As they get more involved with drugs, they need to make "contacts," to meet people who will sell them drugs. You cannot do this by hanging around your "straight" friends. You have got to start associating with other users and people who are regularly in the business of breaking the law. That is the really dangerous part.

We have talked about the no-no's, smoking, drinking, sex and drugs, and some of the reasons for kids being involved with these no-no's. We have also talked, in this chapter as well as in Chapter X, about how to raise kids in a way so as to prevent these areas from becoming problems. What do you do when you discover your kid already has a problem in one of these areas?

The first, and by far the most important step, is to face it squarely. Do not go off "half-cocked," angrily blaming the school system for not teaching your kid how to keep from getting pregnant, or go off with a shotgun in hand after the guy that got your daughter pregnant, or set out to kill those "dope fiends" who have been selling the drugs to your kids. None of that is going to help and, in fact, it will only make matters worse.

Also, it is important not to play games, like "detective." If you suspect your kid is involved in drugs, tell him and tell him why you are concerned. Do not holler or hit or get hysterical, but sit down and talk about it; you know, like "adults." At that point threatening, too, will probably make matters worse. Try to understand and put an end to the problem rather than to punish and take revenge. A good place to start is for you and your spouse to have a good long talk alone, and perhaps by using this book and the "Rules," try to figure out where you have made some mistakes and try to rectify them. For example, if you discover you have been fighting battles you cannot win, just stop fighting and that will help greatly.

The next step is to get other people involved. All too often when we discover our child is having a problem, we are so worried about "what the neighbors will think" or that our boss will find out, that we do not handle the situation wisely, and even sometimes try to cover it up. Covering it up will not make it go away. There are literally thousands of people in every community who would genuinely like to help you with your problem. They range from the school teacher, the counselor, the family minister, the juvenile court worker, various social and family agencies, as well as physicians and psychiatrists. Once again, do not try to hide the problem once you have discovered it; do not hide it from your spouse or your kids or the professionals who are willing and able to help you. Seek help and do not stop until the problem is genuinely solved.

CHAPTER XII

Lying and Stealing

In this chapter and the following chapter on delinquency, I would like to show you how lying and stealing start out to be very innocent, and even natural acts, that if handled incorrectly, go on to create some serious problems in childhood, and may even go on to delinquency as a way of life. This chapter and the next chapter on delinquency differ only in degree. Whether your kid has stolen for the first time, whether it has become a real problem in your family, or whether it has gone on to a way of life for your kid, the causes behind it are frequently the same. In fact, the whole point of this book is to help you as parents prevent the everyday kind of minor problems like lying and stealing from becoming major problems or life long habits.

Why do kids lie and steal the first time? In the paragraph above I said these acts start out very innocently or even naturally. What do I mean? Picture, if you will, a caveman who walked the earth thousands of years ago. Many things he did were "natural" for him. If he were walking along stalking a saber toothed tiger and suddenly felt the urge to pee, he would naturally pee where he found himself. There were not any social taboos against that so he just did it. Or perhaps if he had the instinctual urge to have intercourse, he just found a female and dragged her off and satisfied himself. If you look at it in this way, stealing is a very natural thing to do. If our caveman had been admiring a club belonging to one of his neighbors, he probably would have waited till his neighbor left his cave, and very simply gone in and taken it. He admired something that belonged to somebody else, had an instinctual drive to possess it himself, so he just satisfied that instinct by taking it.

So it is with little children today, and unfortunately many adults. When a two-year-old little boy is admiring his older brother's toy truck, he instinctively wants it for his own and will automatically set out to get it in the easiest way. And the easiest way frequently is by taking it. This is all pretty simple and logical so far, but what throws the monkey wrench into the works are the taboos we have built up in our society. Over thousands and thousands of years we have learned that taking something that belongs to somebody else does not work out very well, so society has taught its children that stealing is wrong. But now we have a conflict. The conflict is that the little boy wants something, but cannot simply get away with taking it or he will get into trouble. He has to find other ways, socially acceptable ways, of getting the toy truck for himself. Through parents teaching him, and through his own experience, he will learn there are other ways of getting things he wants, but yet will not get him into trouble. For instance, the little boy might ask his big brother if he can play with the truck, or he might ask his parents if they will buy a truck for him. The point I am trying to make is that we all have instincts to lie and to steal. The way we learn to get things in a socially acceptable way is by how our parents handle us when we first attempt to lie or steal.

Once again you are rediscovering a major theme of this book; kids are not born with problems. They have their own little traits that may add to problems, such as stubbornness or aggressiveness, but for the most part kids develop problems because of the way we parents handle or mishandle them.

Let me tell you about a case that nicely demonstrates how stealing can start out as an innocent act and then, if it is mishandled, can progress to a chronic problem in early adolescence, and then further progress to full delinquency as a way of life. Let me diagram this pattern:

Stage I		Stage II		Stage III
The First Innocent Theft	mishandled ⟶ by parents	Problem Stealing	mishandled ⟶ by parents	Hard core Delinquency

I first saw Sherry when she was nineteen years old while she was awaiting trial for armed robbery. Sherry was an attractive girl who was very pleasant and personable and, in fact, seemed frighteningly like "the girl next door." But noticeable almost immediately was the fact that she was an angry girl. Her attorney asked me to do a psychiatric evaluation on her because he was looking for a way to get her off the charges. She was obviously quite guilty. It seems Sherry and her boyfriend had recently held up a liquor store and they were arrested in trying to make their escape. I remember all too well her attorney commenting to me, "She just doesn't seem like the type."

I decided to study this case thoroughly because not only was Sherry so interesting, but she represented a classic picture of so many kids I have seen before, kids that have come from nice families and have gone sour. I spent many hours interviewing Sherry, her parents and many people she had known while growing up. Let me run through her life with you, pointing out some important highlights which led up to her present problem.

Sherry was born of middle class, "good parents" who were frighteningly like you and me. Probably their only fault in raising her was they tried too hard. Sherry's mother, in particular, was a pretty uptight lady. She had very strong moralistic attitudes and frequently overreacted to many things Sherry did. Sherry's parents remembered the very first time Sherry had "stolen" something. I would have called it "taken" something, but her parents referred to it as her having "stolen." It was a very innocent situation. When Sherry was four years old she took some candy from a candy dish at home that had been put away "only for company." This is a good example of how innocent and natural the first incident can be.

Her mother got very upset with her. She screamed and hollered at Sherry and in fact got somewhat hysterical. Her mother called her many things like "thief," grabbed the candy away from her, shook her and then spanked her. Remember what I said about how we advertise our sore spots to our kids. It was almost as if Sherry's mother were holding up a sign to her saying "stealing is my sore spot, so if you ever want to get back at me, that's the way to do it."

You can probably guess what happened next. Sherry started taking things from around the house, loose change that was laying around, food and other items of little value such as cheap jewelry belonging to her mother. She probably did not even want the things; she had no use for them since she was given a nice allowance, always had plenty to eat and certainly could not wear the jewelry she had taken. The point is, she was now doing it just to get back at her mother. And of course, each and every time Sherry would take something, her mother would go to the same extremes of overreaction.

This pattern continued over a period of several years and was by far the greatest problem in the family. It is interesting that Sherry's parents took her to see a school psychologist when she was about ten years old. The psychologist at once recognized the "game" that was going on in the family; that Sherry would steal and the parents would react, then Sherry would steal again and the parents would react again, and so on. It was a vicious cycle by then. According to Sherry's parents, the psychologist explained to them how the cycle was going round and round and that they had to stop overreacting to break the cycle. Mother remembered arguing with the psychologist that, "I can't just ignore it, or she'll grow up to be a criminal." When in fact as you can see, it was Mom's "not ignoring it" that was causing the problem.

There was one particular incident that really pointed out very clearly what the problem was, but Sherry's parents were unable to see it and change their actions. You will notice I said change *their* actions. In order for the problem to be solved, Sherry would have to change her actions too. But, whenever two sides are fighting (Sherry and her parents) we must expect the most mature side (hopefully the parents) can stop fighting first. Remember how I said it takes two to fight. If Sherry's parents had stopped, then Sherry would have stopped.

The incident took place when Sherry was fourteen years old. The stealing had continued and each time Sherry's parents had continued to overreact to it. Sherry's mother came from a well-respected family in town. Sherry, her mother and her grandparents had all grown up in that town. There was a particular department store in town where the family was well-known. In fact, whenever Sherry's mother would go to the store to do her shopping, the salesgirls referred to her by name. Two days after a fight between Sherry and her mother, Sherry walked into that department store and went from one department to the next picking up things, putting them under her coat, and openly putting some rings on her finger and jewelry around her neck. What could have been more obvious? She was not only trying to get caught, but trying to do it in a place where her mother was so well-known and respected. This was Sherry's ultimate slap in the face for her mother. Of course the store detective noticed her, the police were called and, as a result, Sherry was placed in a juvenile home for several months. From then on it was all down hill. Sherry was in and out of juvenile homes and finally "made the big time" by holding up a liquor store when she was nineteen.

This is a tragic story for many reasons. First of all it was entirely preventable. If Sherry's mother had not overreacted to Sherry's stealing when she was four, Sherry probably would not have repeated it.

The other thing is that these were all really good people. These parents loved their daughter, they gave her everything including good teaching, but they overdid it; they tried too hard.

I have seen hundreds of examples of lying that start out just as innocently and become a tragic problem. As a matter of fact, we frequently force our kids to lie. How often have you caught your kid doing something wrong and shouted, "Why did you do that?" Probably at the same time you were hovering over him looking very angry and perhaps even threatening him with your hand. He does not know why he did it. But he knows if he does not come up with an answer pretty quick, he is liable to get hurt. So he makes up an answer.

Or how about the kid that comes in the house and tells his parents he saw a house turned upside down from a storm and his parents react and call him a liar? He was not really lying, he was sharing his fantasy or his daydream with his parents. But his parents have a terrible fear that if they do not stop the little lies, he will grow up to be a big liar. They overreact and holler and hit, hoping to change him, but they only make him worse. Would it not be so much better to overlook the fantasies or to simply say, "I doubt that"? And would it not be better to erase that word "Why" from your vocabulary when you are talking to your kids? They really do not know the reasons "why" they do things so why ask them?

As I mentioned in the chapter on discipline, there is probably a very direct relationship between overreacting (whether it be hollering or hitting) and whether kids repeat their bad behavior. In particular there are studies that demonstrate that with stubborn kids and predelinquent kids, punishment encourages their bad behavior to continue.

We frequently set bad examples as parents. Remember the guy who took home a typewriter and then tried to justify it to himself on the basis that they probably would not miss it or they were not paying him enough? And how often we lie to our kids. Usually it is accidental, and we do it automatically. I was recently talking to a set of parents about their hyperactive kid. The week before I had started their kid on medicine to help with his behavior. This week the parents were telling me their little boy did not like the idea of taking his "vitamins" anymore. I asked them what they were talking about, and they said they had told their son that the pills were vitamin pills. I asked these parents why they did that and what was so interesting

was they did not really know. It certainly would not have been harmful for them to tell their son the medicine was to help him control
himself a little better. These parents had lied to their son so automatically they did not even think about it. And, as a matter of fact, they
had lied with all the best intentions. But a lie is a lie.

Many parents lie because they are uncomfortable. Let us suppose
your seven-year-old daughter is reading a magazine and asks, "Daddy,
what is a homosexual?" Of course I think you should explain it to
her as directly and honestly as you can. But there are many parents
who would get very uncomfortable at that point and would give her
some dishonest explanation just to get her to drop the subject.

Let us suppose your kids are very small and they have not yet had
the occasion to lie or steal for the first time. Keep in mind there is an
excellent chance they are going to lie and steal at least a couple of
times in their young lives. How can you prevent it from becoming a
problem? The answer is very simple. When it happens, keep your
cool and do not overreact. Before it actually does happen, you might
want to say to your kids that "we don't take things that don't belong
to us" or "it's very important to tell the truth." But it is probably going to happen anyway, so be prepared for it. The first few times you
catch your kid saying something that is not true or catch him with
something that does not belong to him, calmly say something like, "I
think you took that from your sister, so give it back to her. Remember, Joey, how I always tell you that we do not take things that belong to other people."

You are probably uncomfortable because you are thinking that is
too easy, that you have not scared him into not doing it again. But
remember what I have said repeatedly, you do not motivate good behavior by scaring kids or making them feel guilty. *They will behave
properly to please you.*

Lies should be handled in very much the same way. As a matter
of fact, because many lies are just your kid's fantasies, they could be
ignored and nothing needs to be said. If you do catch your kid in a
blatant lie, however, it is a good idea to say something like, "I don't
think it really happened that way," or "I don't think that is quite
true." If you can leave it at that, I promise you will have a much
better chance of preventing lying and stealing from ever becoming
a problem.

There is one particular problem that puzzles many parents. What

do you do if you are not really sure your kid has told a lie or has actually taken something? Keep in mind you are a parent, not a judge
and a jury all combined. You do not have to have absolute evidence
to have a conviction. Of course I am not at all suggesting to go
around accusing your kids of lying and stealing just because you have
some vague idea they had something to do with it. If you are pretty
sure your kid has taken something, tell him you suspect him and you
are going to act as though he did take it. Let us suppose you find this
shiny new one-dollar bill in your five-year-old's possession, just like
the one-dollar bill that is missing from your wallet. You do not need
to give him a lie detector test or start looking for latent fingerprints.
You can just say to him, "Bill, I found this dollar in your drawer
and I think you took it from my wallet. Remember, I said that we
don't take things that don't belong to us so I'm going to take it back."
He will probably come up with a story about finding it on the way
home from school or having gotten it by selling comic books to a
friend, but just ignore those excuses. Sometimes kids start lying to
cover up stealing. It is bad enough that he has one problem (stealing); do not pursue the issue and make him a liar too.

What do you do if your kids are a little further along than just the
first time with lying and stealing? Probably the best place to begin is
to sit down with your spouse, and both having read this book very
carefully, talk about what is going on in the total family picture. In
particular, of course, you need to ask yourselves things like Rule 1,
have you been fighting battles, or Rule 4, have you been suppressing
your kid's direct anger, and if you have been overreacting to previous
lying and stealing.

Take a long look at your family and sort of "take inventory" on
how things are going. Suppose your son has been doing a lot of lying,
but after reading this book you realize you have been doing a lot of
things wrong. Of course the first place to start is for you and your
spouse to set out to really change yourselves first. You may realize
you need to stop fighting some battles you can't win or you may need
to stop overreacting to the lying or you may need to take some walls
down. Fine, that is an excellent start. Please keep in mind however,
that just because you have changed a pattern that has been going for
a long time, your kid might not change that quickly. Even though
you successfully stop overreacting, he probably is going to lie a few
more times just to test you to see if you really have calmed down and

his lying is not getting to you anymore. Be patient and wait. The change in him will come if you have truly changed first.

I am not at all trying to give you the idea that this book is "do-it-yourself family therapy." I still believe strongly in the importance of using the professionals in your community who are willing and able to help you with your problems. But I think the book is an excellent place to start and I honestly feel that you can probably solve the majority of problems on your own without ever having to seek professional advice.

CHAPTER XIII

Delinquency

This chapter will be meaningless to you unless you have read Chapter XII. Delinquency is nothing more than a point farther along the same continuum as lying and stealing. In the previous chapter I stressed how bad behavior can start out innocently and so "naturally." I further showed you how overreacting to it causes it to continue and get worse. When I use the term delinquency I am thinking about a situation in which usually a teen-ager or young adult has developed a pattern of behavior that has become a way of life for him. It is no longer a small problem that gets him in trouble with his parents, but it has spread to school, to other people outside his family and to the community at large.

Very frequently by the time a kid becomes delinquent, his original reasons for it are no longer present. In the last chapter, by the time Sherry was arrested for armed robbery she was no longer living at home, and as a matter of fact, had not seen her mother for a couple of years. She was not stealing any more to get back at her mother; rather she was just doing it because it became a habit. Many habits start out with some pretty good reasons but just end up as habits. Many of us started smoking to look big or impress the other kids. When we are thirty-five and still smoking we are not doing it to impress the other kids, we are just doing it because it is a habit and it sort of continues on its own. It is the same with delinquent behavior. It frequently can start out accidentally and then become a tool to get back at parents or rattle their cages. If the vicious cycle is allowed to continue, it can develop into a way of life all by itself.

Some psychiatrists would define a delinquent as a kid who does not have a conscience; he has no sense of right and wrong. I find this to be a very narrow definition, and as a matter of fact, I have seen only a very few kids, of the total number of kids that I have seen in trouble, who really do not have much of a sense of right and wrong. The large majority of kids in trouble can tell you what they are doing is wrong and can even feel guilty about it, but it has become such a habit with them that they cannot break it. Again an example might be the smoker who has smoked for many years out of habit. He knows it is wrong, he knows it is going to get him into trouble someday, but he feels powerless to stop himself.

The term delinquent is really a description of kids who are having a variety of serious behavior problems ranging from lying and stealing, to other forms of breaking the law. If we wanted to, we could break these kids into categories based on the reasons behind their getting in trouble. Perhaps the first category then would be largely the group I described in the last chapter, the kid who starts out getting back at his parents or uses stealing as a way of expressing his anger, but ends up doing it just because it has become a well-ingrained habit.

The second group would be the kid who, from the beginning, has never really learned a sense of right and wrong. This might be a kid who is raised in the underworld, perhaps his father being part of the "syndicate." He certainly is taught a sense of right and wrong, but it is not the same sense of right and wrong that you and I are taught. He is taught that it is all right to kill as long as he is doing it to someone outside the "family." He probably is also taught it is all right to lie and steal so long as you do that also outside the "family." This kid does develop a sense of right and wrong, but his values are very different from the larger society.

I have talked with many parents, particularly in the ghettoes, who teach their kids that it is all right to steal, but they just should not get caught. A couple of years ago I was very embarrassed when I heard something come out of my own mouth that I had not intended. My daughters and I were watching a news program about the increase of crime in major cities in the United States, particularly stealing. At that time I said to my daughters, "Don't ever let me catch you stealing." In this statement I was accidentally implying that it is all right to steal, but not to get caught.

A third category of delinquents are kids who *accidentally* are encouraged to become delinquent. All of us tend to encourage our kids to do things we were unable to do, and there is probably nothing wrong with that so long as we are aware of what we are doing. For instance, I always wanted to play the piano when I was a kid, but never did, so I have been encouraging my daughters to get interested in the piano. It is as American as apple pie to want our kids to have more and do more than we did as kids. But where we get into trouble is when we unknowingly (accidentally) encourage our kids to do things that we were never allowed to do in our childhood.

There are two notable examples that come to mind, and I see these and many others come up frequently in my practice. The first is the lady who was raised in a strict religious family and was never able to experiment with sex. She married a very proper gentleman at a fairly early age and missed out on the "running around years" that many women secretly wish for. When this lady has a teenage daughter of her own she unknowingly or unwittingly encourages her daughter to act out some of the sexual experiences she wished she could have had. Again she does not say to her daughter, "Go out and have as much fun as you can." She does it in a much more subtle way so that she is not even aware herself she is doing it. She might do it by not giving her daughter a time to be in the house following a date, or by letting her go off to a slumber party which she knows will be un-chaperoned.

Another common example I see is the father who was raised in a very strict household where he was never allowed to fight and get into the usual kind of trouble boys get into. When his own son comes along and starts getting into fights, this dad is liable to sit back and say, "My, he's all boy," rather than stopping the fights or disciplining his son for them. He further might turn his head, knowing that the boy is off with the gang, "up to no good."

A fourth reason why some kids become delinquent is that some-body in their lives, usually a parent, has really let them get away with a great deal. These are the kids we usually refer to as "spoiled" kids or "wild" kids. Sometimes parents feel very guilty about the past and for that reason tend to let their kids get away with a lot of things, "to make it up to them." A set of parents may have their first child and after a year or two decide that being a parent is a real pain. They find that having kids is not all it is cracked up to be and further de-cide not to have any more kids. It is pretty hard for any of us to face those kinds of feelings, although we all have them at some time in our lives, especially after a bunch of messy diapers or after dad has been babysitting with the kids while mom is shopping. These feelings are pretty hard to accept, and we sometimes go overboard. We try to make up for not loving the kid enough by treating him better or even spoiling him, and of course that does not produce anything but one spoiled kid.

Perhaps there are other reasons we are feeling guilty and then try to ' make it up to the kid." Maybe dad is an alcoholic so mom tries to be both mother and father. Or this may be an adopted child who, through no fault of the current parents, was deprived of some early love and attention. Do not misunderstand, it is fine to give a lot of love to a deprived child, but do not mistake love for not setting limits. As a matter of fact, *controlling your child and setting limits for him is a very special kind of love.*

It disturbs me greatly how many of the "new intellectual" set are raising their kids so permissively. I am reminded of a family who lived in our neighborhood a few years ago. Dad was a young, very bright attorney and mother had her master's degree in psychology. When their six-year-old daughter would come over to our house to visit, she was so wild and uncontrollable that, as much as we hated to do it, my wife and I finally said she would not be allowed in our house anymore. We found many of our neighbors felt that way too and also had imposed similar restrictions. The lawyer and his wife somehow had the funny idea that controlling their daughter might limit her precious intelligence. It was tragic, but what they were unintentionally doing was allowing their daughter to develop bad patterns of behavior which were hurting her very much in her present life and would continue to hurt her in her future life. After all, who wants to be friends with a spoiled brat. It is the same kind of extreme permissiveness that also can lead to delinquency.

I would like to remind you about Rule 2 which says, "Always follow through and be consistent." In that rule I mentioned how mom might make a one week restriction for her daughter and might not tell dad about it. Perhaps halfway through the week's restriction dad would come along and let his daughter off. Further I said that all they were really accomplishing was teaching their daughter how to cheat the system and teaching her how to manipulate it and get away with things. If we let our kids manipulate their way out of the rules we have at home, they will learn to manipulate society's rules.

The fifth major cause of delinquency, as I have already discussed in Chapter XII, is the parent who, knowingly or unknowingly, sets bad examples for his kids. Again we may think we are not going to influence our kids, but we do. As one parent said to me, "But gee, Doc, I only cheat a little bit on my income tax." We happened to be discussing this man's ten-year-old son who had developed the habit of cheating during examinations at school. This father had been so sure his son knew nothing about his income tax and yet when I interviewed the boy privately he filled my ears with stories of Dad's cheating (in more ways than just financially).

Because of the serious nature of delinquency, we usually need a great deal of professional help when things have gotten this far. The tragedy in the United States is that for the most part, help is not available. As a psychiatric consultant to juvenile courts for a number of years, I have been terribly disappointed at the lack of adequate services for teenagers. Certainly the services for adults are nothing to write home about, but you would think our society would be interested in doing more for teenagers to prevent them from becoming "adult offenders" two or three years later. But we do not. Juvenile courts for the most part do not handle kids until they are in terribly serious trouble and by that time it is usually too late. How often I have had parents come to me and tell me they went to the juvenile court because their kid was doing a fair amount of petty lying and stealing, and the courts told them they could not help them until the kid committed some major theft. I am not blaming the courts themselves. For the most part they are handicapped by us taxpayers. We spend billions of dollars to put men on the moon and are unwilling to spend a few dollars to keep our kids out of jail.

The juvenile courts suffer from an "image problem." Many people have the same attitude about the juvenile court that they have about police. That is most unfortunate. The juvenile court was not developed to "put it to your kid." It was developed to help all of us. Certainly there can come a time for any of us when we, as parents, will not be able to control our kids and we will have to turn to some other, more powerful, authority to control them. I see so many parents that should be breaking down the door of the juvenile court to get their help who tell me, "I'm not going to turn in my own kid."

As you have probably seen from reading this chapter, no delinquent kid is a pure strain. He is probably a combination of many of the causes and situations that lead up to delinquency. Certainly the emotional or psychological factors are a major contribution to delinquency and yet psychiatric facilities in the United States are also pathetically inadequate for teenagers. Fifteen years ago I toured my first big psychiatric hospital. I was so upset by the degradation I saw, the inadequate treatment and facilities and particularly seeing young teenagers on wards with two hundred crazy adults, that I came home and threw up. As a matter of fact, I was not able to keep any food down for the next two and one-half days. I think it would be an excellent experience for every citizen in the community to tour the local penal and psychiatric facilities, particularly those for teenagers. You will never be complacent again.

When kids reach the stage of delinquency, things have frequently gone too far for you as parents to help them or control them. That is why we must insist on better community and state facilities for treatment and control.

CHAPTER XIV

School Problems

What I would like to do in this chapter is to try to give you a way of looking at school problems. Sometimes when our kids have problems in school, we have a hard time seeing the forest for the trees—the problem seems to be one big amorphous blob. This chapter will hopefully put you on the right track to defining, understanding and then solving your child's school problem. This can best be accomplished by working hand-in-hand with your child's teacher(s) and counselor.

Let me try and simplify the whole business by making a diagram for you:

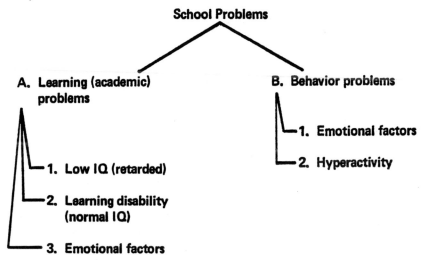

Whether you are a parent or a teacher, a good way of looking at school problems is to divide them up into two main categories—learning problems and behavior problems. Certainly some kids will have both, but for the most part they usually have much more of one than the other. It helps us to understand the reasons for their problems if we break them down into these two major areas. You are sitting there wondering about your own kid who is having some problems in school. Think for a minute, is the problem *mainly* that he has a hard time learning or are most of the problems you hear about related to his bad behavior. If you can make this distinction, then you are on the way to helping him.

Let us take a look at the three major subcategories for the learning or academic problems. What things keep kids from learning? First of all there is the kid who just does not have the IQ or the intelligence. He is a good kid, he tries hard, but he just does not have what it takes and he cannot be expected to keep up with the regular classroom. This determination is made not only by you as parents watching how he does in his growing up years, but mostly by school people who have observed him and given him some basic IQ tests. Retarded kids make up about three percent of the total school-age population. I have set aside the next chapter to talk in more detail about the retarded kid because I think he has some unique problems that his parents must help him deal with.

A second group of kids that have a hard time learning are called learning disabilities. Unlike the retarded kids, they have a normal IQ. They seem to be trying very hard, but they just do not get it. Frequently their parents and teachers tell us that the kid seems to be very smart in certain areas, like using his hands or figuring out math problems, but he still has a terrible time with reading or spelling. There are many different names for this category. Sometimes they are called learning disabilities, sometimes they are said to have perceptual-motor problems, sometimes they are referred to as minimumly brain-damaged or dyslexic. These kids make up about ten percent of the school-aged population.

I find it helpful to think of learning disabilities in the following way: Suppose you are sitting in your living room and you look up at the wall and see that one of the pictures on the wall is crooked. You stand up and walk over there and straighten it. You probably did not realize it, but you have just completed a very, very intricate circuit. Let us go back over that circuit again. The image is transmitted from the crooked picture on the wall to your eye by light waves. The image goes into your eye and gets carried by the nerves of your eye up to your brain. Your brain is like a computer and that image registers on your computer and your computer tries to make some sense out of it. By past experience your computer knows the picture is crooked and knows something must be done about it. Your computer sends the message down your spinal cord in your back, out through the nerves to the muscles of your arms and legs and activates them. You stand up, walk over to the wall, reach up and straighten the picture.

That is so simple and automatic that we do not even think about it, but that is because we do not have perceptual-motor problems. Many kids do have these problems, particularly when they are young. This fancy circuit is called a perceptual-motor circuit because it includes everything from the time you see (perceive) the picture on the wall to the time you finally get up and move your muscles (motor) to straighten it. Anything going wrong anywhere in that circuit can mess up the whole circuit. If your vision is poor and you do not see the picture, obviously you cannot complete the circuit. Or if you have a paralyzed leg and cannot walk over to the picture, you also will not be able to complete the circuit. These parts are relatively easy to understand. If our kids are not learning because they cannot see or because they cannot hear, we frequently can pick up these problems quite easily with some simple hearing and vision tests. Or if a kid cannot write because his hand is not working properly, we frequently know very early. But where the real difficulty comes in is when that computer does not work right. The kid with a computer problem might be able to see okay and would notice that the picture's crooked. And if he can walk okay and move his muscles all right he will be able to straighten it. Where the hitch comes in is that the idea of the picture being crooked does not register in his mind. This is a difficult thing for all of us, whether we are parents or professionals, to understand. As a matter of fact professionals disagree with each other all the time over these learning disability problems and rarely will two professionals agree on the meaning of terms like perceptual-motor or learning disabilities. What is most important to remember is that, if your kid is having some trouble in school, one possible reason and something that needs to be looked into, is that he may have a learning disability. Something may be going wrong in that intricate circuit which is made up of his five senses, his brain and his motor system.

You are probably wondering how kids get these learning disabilities. This is a handicap of the brain. Although this kid is of normal intelligence, something is actually wrong with his brain. Either it did not develop quite right, or most likely what happened was that during the delivery the brain did not get enough oxygen and some of the brain cells were damaged. Do not get all panicky over that term "brain damaged." We are all born with about four billion brain cells, and we can certainly afford to eliminate a few without getting into serious trouble. It just depends on which few you bump off. With many kids who have this problem, there is a history of a difficult delivery, the kid's not breathing immediately after delivery or perhaps there was an Rh (blood type) problem that caused some of his brain cells to be knocked off. Sometimes the problem comes a little later on in the child's life when perhaps he may have a high fever, some infection of his brain (encephalitis or meningitis) or a head injury. Some professionals feel learning disabilities tend to run in families (hereditary). In still other kids who have these learning disabilities, we cannot find any reason why it happened; it just happened.

If your kid's behavior in the classroom and at home is just fine, but academically he is not doing very well, the next thing to do is to talk to his teacher(s) and counselor. They can help you to find out which of the three major reasons is causing his academic difficulty. A few simple IQ tests will tell you if he is retarded, and his teacher(s) and counselor will probably have a good idea if he is having these academic problems for emotional reasons. A counselor or school psychologist can now be a big help by giving him some special tests to help define more carefully the kind of problem he is having academically. Also keep in mind your family doctor or pediatrician can be very helpful too in finding reasons for his academic difficulty. To make a diagnosis of learning disability the three important steps will be talking with the teacher and counselor, getting a complete physical and mental examination and special psychological tests.

Suppose you do all these things and the professionals tell you that your kid has a learning disability. That may mean something or it may not mean much, depending on how severe his case is. Very frequently kids, without any special kind of help, either outgrow this condition or learn to compensate for it. For example, imagine you were born without your right middle finger. Then suppose at about age ten or twelve you started to learn how to type. At first it would be quite difficult for you because you are missing that right middle finger. But after a while your other fingers would learn to hit the keys your right middle finger would have ordinarily hit; they would learn to compensate for its absence. So it is with our brain. Even though we bump off a few cells at birth or when we are very young, very frequently the other billions of cells can learn to compensate for the few that are damaged. Brain cells never grow back once they are killed, but other brain cells probably take over for the dead ones. Things may get better on their own without any special help.

Sometimes special instructions may be needed or perhaps some special perceptual-motor training. But leave that up to the professionals to decide. As you have noticed in my discussing learning disabilities, most diagnostic and treatment work has to be up to the professional people. I am mentioning it in this chapter for the sake of completeness and so you will know a little bit more about this important reason for kids not doing well in school.

Let us take a look now at the third category for why kids have a hard time learning; that is the group who does not learn for emotional reasons. Remember I am talking about kids with normal intelligence and kids who do not have any of the learning disability problems that I just talked about. It has seemed to me that every one of these kids that I have seen was just getting back at his parents by using school as a club. For years I kept telling myself it must be more complicated than this, so I have read everything I could get my hands on concerning school and why kids do not learn. And you know something? It really is that simple! No matter how you phrase it, no matter in what fancy terms you put it, *bright kids who are not cutting it in school have something going on at home.* It is that simple.

Picture dropping a stone in the middle of a swimming pool. The ripples go out in circles, getting bigger and bigger until the ripples finally reach the edge of the pool. The bigger the stone, the bigger the ripples that reach the edges of the pool. It is the same with families. There might be a disturbance anywhere in the family; dad and mom could be having some quarrels, teenage daughter may be running away. But whatever is going on, everybody in the family is going to feel it, and everybody is going to react to it in their own special way. The bigger the problem, the farther away it will be felt. It starts out with the person himself feeling it, then his immediate family, then friends and school, then the community at large.

A family I saw recently is like thousands of other families, where one of the kids is having problems in learning. Fred was an eight-year-old third grader who was referred to me by the school because he seemed to be having a great deal of difficulty learning. School information revealed that Fred had been tested up one side and down the other. His intelligence tests were always slightly above normal, there was no evidence of any learning disability, and numerous check-ups by the family doctor revealed nothing of a physical nature. Fred just was not learning, and the school and the parents were stumped.

My interviewing Fred did not add much to the picture. He was a nice-looking young lad who seemed alert and intelligent, but admitted that he was not very fond of school. We talked for half an hour about other areas of his life and that too was not particularly revealing. When I interviewed Fred's parents, however, I found what I was looking for. They were good parents who worked very hard as parents (perhaps too hard). They felt strongly about Fred's getting a good education. In fact they were pushing him too hard. They insisted Fred sit down each evening and do an hour's work, and they did lots of other things like check his homework and made Fred read to them. What he really liked to do was to be out there playing baseball, and he felt he was always being punished, but he was not sure for what.

The other problem going on in the family was a discipline one. Fred not only got spanked for his lousy grades, but there was a fair amount of spanking and strict discipline for many things including Fred's not keeping his room clean, his not wanting to eat and his "being disrespectful" to his parents. In other words, Fred's parents were on him a lot. He was getting harassed about his grades and his behavior, and it seemed to Fred that he was getting harassed about everything. What can an eight-year-old boy do about a situation like that? In his family he certainly could not go to his dad and tell him to back off or tell mom to stop bugging him. He knew what would happen if he did. But there was an answer. He could show dad who would be the boss over how he did in school, and at the same time rattle mom and dad's cage a little for having rattled his. What a beautiful solution. He could just do badly in school, and he could get back at both of them. Now I do not mean to imply Fred thought this all out consciously or deliberately, but what is the difference? He was still doing badly in school and that was the reason for it.

Remember how I said earlier in the book that "kids fight dirty"? If your wife smashes the car, probably you and your wife will really get into it over the car. But kids are much more subtle, and they get back at us indirectly. If you fight with your kid over keeping his room clean, he is not going to be so stupid as to fight back with you in that same area, that is by leaving his room a mess. You would probably figure that out, and he would be in trouble if you thought he were just thumbing his nose at you. He fights dirty; he fights back in an area that is so unrelated you do not even realize it is happening. He fights back by doing badly in school. This is the reason kids do poorly in school. Because somebody's fighting with them and they are going to poke you with that thing called school and watch you squirm.

All the things we have been talking about in these few paragraphs concerning emotional reasons certainly apply to kids who are having behavioral problems in school as well as academic ones. Why do some kids take it out in behavior and some others take it out by getting poor grades? Kids are just different.

Remember in Rule 3 I talked about the uncanny ways our kids trick us into giving them attention. This is particularly important when we are talking about school problems. How often when it comes to school do we really reward our kid's bad behavior rather than stop it? When a kid is goofing off at home while he is supposed to be doing his homework and you go into his room and start going over the homework with him, you have just rewarded his misbehavior by giving him attention. I think it is much better that if he does not do his homework, he has to face the teacher the next day.

Or how about the kid who has developed a lifelong habit at home of getting his parent's attention by misbehaving? If it worked at home, it will probably work in school, and so he is going to try it there too. Many kids are disruptive in the classroom because it works; it gets them a lot of attention. If every time they jump up from their chair or throw a spitball the teacher reacts to it, they are being rewarded by her attention and they love every minute of it. If they can get tutored in the evening by their parents for not learning in school, they are probably going to continue not learning. After all, what kid could turn down several hours of attention from his parents in the evening? It is just too good to resist.

What do you do if your kid is having trouble in school for an emotional reason? Remember Rules 1, 3 and 4. You will probably in reading them find something you are doing drastically wrong. When you recognize what you are doing wrong, set about to change it. I have counseled many, many parents who have discovered they are fighting battles they cannot win or are accidentally rewarding bad

behavior with their attention or are keeping their kids from expressing their anger directly and therefore having the kid take it out in
school. Once we have discovered what the problem is, the rest is
pretty simple.

Let me describe to you what I think is a good approach for any
parent to take to prevent school problems. Sit down with your kid
when he starts school, talk to him about the importance of paying
attention and learning all he can because getting a good education
will help him later on. As he goes along you are going to expect him
to do well, you are going to praise him when he brings home good
papers and good report cards and in general you are going to show
you are very pleased with his doing well in school. When he brings
home bad grades or bad report cards you are going to tell him you
are unhappy with that and you expect him to improve. If he does
not improve right away you are not going to punish him or get into
any battles over his grades. In other words, you will be "using the
carrot instead of the stick." Nobody ever forced his kid to learn. It
cannot be done, so you encourage him. *He will do his best to please
you.* Do not get into the business of paying him off with money or
toys; your pleasure with him is his best reward.

But suppose you have already · had some problems for many
years and you discover you have been fighting battles over grades and
think now you would like to stop. Fine, stop immediately. As I said
before, I think it is all right to change horses in the middle of the
stream providing you tell your kid you are doing it. If you have been
bugging him about his grades and his homework for years and you are
going to change, that is fine—providing you let him know you are
going to do it. You might tell him somethnig like, "Look, Fred, this is
kind of silly. For years you and I have been going round and round
over your grades and that hasn't helped a bit. Remember I said your
grades are going to help you in later life, so Mom and I are going to
make it your responsibility. From now on your grades are going to be
completely up to you."

Keep in mind what I said earlier about kids having to test us. Probably for the next grade card or two Fred's grades will get worse. He
will be trying to see if you are really going to stick to what you said
and not do anything about it. If you can stick to that and not react,
then Fred will do something about it. When he sees that you are no

longer going to get upset about it, he will probably start taking more responsibility for his grades himself.

If the problem you are having with your kid in school has more to do with his behavior rather than his grades, I would suggest getting together with the teacher and counselor and use the "Rules" as a guideline to figure out what you are doing wrong. If he is misbehaving, it must be working for him. If his bad behavior no longer works, he will give it up.

The last category of school problems is the kid who is a behavior problem because he is hyperactive. I will discuss this condition more completely in Chapter XIX, but I am mentioning it here for the sake of completeness.

If your child is not yet having problems in school, make his education *his* responsibility. Adopt an "encouraging" rather than a "punishing" approach.

If he is having school problems, decide first if his difficulty is primarily in the area of grades or behavior. In either case, your child's teacher(s) and counselor can help you further define the source of difficulty, and you will be well on your way toward helping your child solve his school problems.

CHAPTER XV

The Retarded Kid

Since the Second World War, there has been a tremendous emphasis in the United States on higher education, particularly towards college and postgraduate training. The GI Bill, the Space Program and many scientific breakthroughs are just a few of the many factors which have led to a national preoccupation with education. Many people in our country today believe education is the ultimate and other things in life are less important.

Most high schools across the United States have excellent programs for college-bound kids, but have few programs to prepare kids to go out in the world after high school. This is particularly tragic when you realize that only about twenty percent of high school kids will go on to college and the vast majority (80%) will need to learn to make their livelihood in ways other than academically.

Fortunately our society has been coming back in recent years to a realization that there are more things to life than just how many degrees you can pile up. If we really think about what we want for our kids, most of us would agree that we want them to be happy, healthy and well-adjusted and to find an area of life in which they can be successful. I am not playing down the importance of education, but I am reminding all of us that there are other ways to achieve the goals I have mentioned other than through education.

No one feels the academic pressures more acutely than retarded kids. As they go through school many retarded kids, if not most, feel increasingly worthless because they cannot keep up with other kids in the academic areas. As parents we frequently allow this to happen by not reminding them that there are other more important things in life like being well-adjusted and happy. Therefore, parents of retarded kids have a particularly difficult task because they must honestly recognize that their kids are never going to "make it" academically and need to help their kids find other areas of success, such as developing manual skills.

What I would like to do in this chapter is to suggest some ways in which parents of retarded kids can help their children find happiness through success at something other than academics. Let us take a look at some of the obstacles parents of retarded kids face as they go along through life.

The first and probably the most important area in which parents of retarded kids run into difficulty is in facing the problem directly. Take a look at an average couple who have a retarded child. They are thirty-five years old, and they already have two normal children, a girl nine and a boy six. Dad has a factory job, and mom is a housewife who is spending most of her time taking care of her family. When their third child is born they are told by the obstetrician that the delivery did not go very well, and the baby's breathing was a bit of a problem and his color was not good at birth. Already the first seeds of doubt have been planted in the minds of the parents. They are wondering what problems might develop later on, but they do not voice their concern. What they should do at that point is talk with their doctor more and ask him specifically if he thinks there is a cause for concern. Many doctors are not very open about their concerns with newborn kids because they sometimes feel it reflects on them as physicians and they too wonder if they could have done anything to prevent the birth problem. You see right off we have a set of parents and a physician who for a variety of reasons are not really talking openly with each other. Many physicians, to prevent undue alarm in the parents, will intentionally "play down" their observations about the child, again which only further leads to forcing the problem underground. As I have stressed, keeping "family secrets" never works out very well.

When little Billy is seventeen months old and still not walking, again his parents are concerned about his being slow to develop so they take him to their pediatrician. The pediatrician, not wanting to be an alarmist, pats the parents on the back and tells them Billy is coming along a little slow, but it is all right and not to worry. Again their concern is forced underground. I am not trying to put all the blame on physicians. Certainly many kids who walk later than fifteen months grow up to be very normal. The problem here is not that Billy is walking late, the problem is that nobody is taking the parents' concerns seriously and discussing them openly with them. Even if the parents' concerns were discussed openly, there is not a lot to do at that point except sit back and wait to see how the kid develops. But at least the parents discussing this with somebody would help allay some of their fears as well as help to plan for future approaches to Billy and his problem.

Another major part of this business of keeping the problem underground is that most of us as parents do not want to face our concerns. None of us would like to think we have a retarded kid at home for many reasons. We worry about the kid's future. We worry about how we are going to provide for him when he is older, and we start to feel guilty about what caused it.

Literally thousands of books have been written on mental retardation, both for the professional and for parents. Thousands of causes of mental retardation have been identified, some of these being passed along through heredity, some being accidents of birth and still many others where there is no known cause. But after all, what is the difference? If you have a retarded kid, it rarely helps to know why it happened. All too often what happens is that one or both parents get in the business of needing to blame someone. They blame themselves, their spouse or the doctor or someone else. That does not help. It only makes matters worse. In fact, parents' blaming somebody is a way for them not to have to face the painful fact that they have a retarded kid. They get so caught up in law suits or divorces that they do not really stop and admit to themselves that they have a retarded child and that they should start planning for him.

Another destructive thing that parents of retarded kids sometimes do is what we call "shopping." They will take their kid to one doctor who tells them that their kid is retarded. They do not want to hear that because it is too painful and too upsetting so they go to another doctor, hoping he will tell them something they want to hear. The next physician tells them the same thing so they move on and on and on from one doctor to the next, from one clinic to the next, from one university center to the next. All too often the shopping goes on for years, and all the time these parents are not really facing the problem and therefore not really helping their kid who, after all, needs more help and understanding than the average kid.

The next major area of difficulty that parents of retarded kids frequently face is when their child reaches school age. They have tried to put the problem out of their minds because they have not wanted to face it. They have not talked with their doctors and they have kept the "family secret." Of course when their kid starts school they do not tell the school about their concerns. Little Billy starts in kindergarten but just does not seem to be keeping up with the other kids. The teacher calls Billy's parents in for a conference, but they keep finding convenient excuses for not making it. The year very quickly goes by. At the end of the year, reading readiness tests, as well as the teacher's opinion show, Billy is not ready for first grade so he repeats kindergarten. At the end of his second time through kindergarten he is still not particularly ready, but he just sort of gets passed on to the first grade. Finally, after many years, the "family secret" can no longer be kept. The school psychologist, counselor and teacher confront Billy's parents with the problem. The parents react by getting angry and blaming the school for not giving Billy a good education. Or perhaps they further try to delay the problem's coming to the surface by asking the school to pass him along and reassuring the school that they "will work with Billy at home in the evening."

In the meantime Billy has spent two years in kindergarten and one year in first grade, all three years of school not having been particularly helpful to him. To make matters worse, throughout these years Billy's parents have been so uncomfortable that they have started overreacting to Billy, causing him to develop some behavior problems. Also over the last three years Billy has come to realize that he just "can't cut it." He has not been able to keep up with the other kids; he knows it, and he feels badly about it. Billy has already started to feel worthless and because the problem has never been discussed openly in the family, Billy's parents cannot reassure him that he is a worthwhile little boy even though he is having trouble at school. Remember I said earlier that kids who feel worthless, tend to act worthless. Billy now has three problems; he is retarded, he is a behavior problem and he has low self-esteem, that is, he feels worthless. As if Billy did not come into the world with enough difficulty being retarded, his parents, by not facing the problem openly and honestly, have helped Billy develop other problems as well.

In the remainder of this chapter I would like to offer you some guidelines to follow with the retarded child to help him grow up healthy, happy and successful.

1. *Accept the fact that you have a retarded kid.* As soon as you suspect your kid may be different, do not hide it; talk openly about it. Discuss it with your spouse, your family doctor, the other children in the family, as well as relatives and friends. Not only will this help you with your feelings about your child, but it will also help you plan in a much better way for him. Remember, keeping the "family secret" will only make matters worse.

2. *The "Rules for Raising Kids" apply to your retarded kid also.* Study the rules carefully and work on them. He was born with one problem, retardation. Do not make him develop other problems as he goes along.

3. *Get some diagnostic tests.* The physician's taking a careful history and doing a thorough physical examination is always the best place to start. There are many tests that can be done to further help define the problem. Many people think IQ tests cannot be done until after the kid is started in school. Of course, the older the kid is, the more accurate the tests are going to be, but even at the age of three, some IQ tests can be given that will give a rough estimate of intelligence and perhaps, potential. Retesting at one or two year intervals is also important to see how things are progressing.

4. *Seek help from agencies.* Besides the usual professionals in your community, there are many agencies that are set up specifically to help retarded kids and their families. The AMA, the National Institute of Mental Health and many other national, state and local agencies will be happy to help you. Write to them and get as much information as you can.

5. *Cooperate with the school people.* They are the best people to help you plan your child's education and training. I am including the following table so you will get an idea where your kid stands with respect to other kids. A good way to do this I think is to divide kids according to IQ and the educational program that will be best for them.

Type of Educational Program	*IQ*
Advanced Program (Superior)	130
Regular Classroom (Normal)	80
Educationally Mentally Handicapped (EMH)	50
Trainable Mentally Handicapped (TMH)	30
Institutional	

6. *Try to locate yourself in a city where there are good school programs for retarded kids.* Try in particular to find a school program that has good vocational training such as auto mechanics, wood shops, cosmetology course, art and music.

7. *Find your kid's areas of success.* We all have areas in which we can do very well and still other areas in which we can be considered retarded. How well I remember buying a new car a few years ago. I am okay when it comes to using my head and my mouth, but I am

essentially retarded when it comes to using my hands. I was washing the car one day and thought I had better check the oil. I looked under the hood for the oil stick, but I could not find it. For three months I looked for that oil stick and found all kinds of other interesting things like the automatic transmission fluid indicator, but never the oil stick. Finally I had to take the car to the corner garage for them to show me where the oil stick was. We all have areas of success and areas of failure.

Do not wait to accidentally stumble across things with which your retarded kid can be successful. Actively seek out areas of success for him. Perhaps he is good at taking things apart or painting or music. Perhaps he excels at getting along with other kids or at sports. Encourage those areas of his life and play down the academic areas.

8. *Try to place reasonable expectations on your kid.* Nothing is more tragic than the parents who demand too much or too little from their retarded kid. Again, the professionals and school people can help you with assessing his capabilities.

9. *Do not get frustrated and give up.* Frustration can be defined as anger we feel in not being able to reach a goal. If you find you get tense and angry when you try to help your retarded kid learn his alphabet or learn to tell time, it would be better not to teach him at all, but rather leave it up to someone else who can keep cool. Do not try *too* hard, you will only get frustrated, and your anger might get in the way of your having a decent relationship with your kid.

10. *Do not go through life wearing a "hair" shirt.* Feeling guilty and punishing yourself for bringing your retarded kid into the world will only make matters worse. Some parents get so caught up in this kind of thinking that they never take vacations or allow themselves real enjoyment of life. All that "self-punishment" will not help.

11. *Do not overprotect your retarded kid.* More than other kids, he needs to learn responsibility and must learn to fend for himself. Overprotecting him will only prevent him from growing to maturity and becoming independent and responsible.

12. *It is perfectly normal to have mixed feelings about your retarded kid.* We all have mixed feelings about our kids regardless of whether they are normal, crippled, retarded or unusual in some other way. There are days that we hate them and days that we love them. It is very normal for you to have mixed feelings about your kid, so allow yourself to have those feelings; do not try to suppress them. Talk

over your mixed feelings with your spouse, your minister and your physician. It helps to air out those feelings.

Fortunately the pendulum in recent years has been swinging back in our society to a place where there is respect for all human beings whether they are smart or retarded, black or white, Catholic or Jew, rich or poor. We are not there yet, but at least we are finally headed in the right direction.

I think the Alcoholics Anonymous prayer is helpful to think about in raising all kids, but in particular, retarded kids:

God grant me the Serenity
to accept the things
I cannot change . . .
Courage to change the things
I can . . .
and the Wisdom to know the difference.

CHAPTER XVI

The Teacher and Behavior

The classroom teacher is the first line of defense against so many problems we have with our kids. She has the advantage of seeing our kids many hours a day, throughout the school year. Parents see their kids many hours a day, but the teacher has the added advantage of not being related to the little fellows. She knows at the end of the day that they will be going home and so will she, and she can get away from the problems at least for a few hours. This frequently gives her the advantage of being much more objective than parents. She can look at the kid over a period of time and evaluate and re-evaluate his personality and his progress. She is often the first one to notice changes in his physical health and often can spot other problems such as emotional problems the kid is having and frequently becomes aware of some family stress the kid is caught up in. She can be of tremendous assistance in evaluating other problems such as learning disabilities, hyperactivity and mental retardation. We therefore need to depend heavily on teachers, not only to educate our kids, but to look at them as total human beings and understand and work with their problems.

I sometimes get upset with teachers when they tell me, "I don't want to be a psychiatrist, I just want to teach." It would be nice if every kid who came into her class was ready to learn. But we must remember teaching is a two-way street; there must be a teacher to teach and a kid to learn. If a kid comes into her classroom suffering from some emotional stress or from a learning disability, he is not going to be in any position to learn and all her fine teaching skills will be wasted. It is terribly important, therefore, for a teacher not "just to teach," but to help her students learn. My purpose in this chapter is to suggest to teachers some ways in which they can help their kids learn.

The Eight Basic Rules in the first part of this book must certainly be understood and practiced by teachers. Many of these rules apply directly to classroom techniques, for instance Rule I which talks about not fighting battles you cannot win. Certainly the other rules have important functions in the classroom too, such as consistency and reinforcing good behavior. As you run through the rules, it will become obvious to you how they apply to the classroom teacher in her relationship with her students. But moreover, the teacher must be well aware of the rules, particularly when the parents of her students are having trouble with them. I have mentioned many times how problems start out quite small, usually within the family, and then gradually spread outside the family to other areas such as school and the community. If a teacher is truly interested in helping kids learn, she will be interested in helping the parents of her students be more successful parents. It is a sad but true fact that universities prepare teachers to teach math and history and other subjects, but do a pathetically inadequate job of helping teachers prepare their students to learn. What all too often happens is the teacher becomes vaguely aware of one of her students having some emotional difficulty. The teacher becomes uncomfortable with the kid because she has had little training or experience in dealing with him or his problems. She then becomes somewhat aloof or detached to protect herself from her own anxiety and frustration. How about the poor student? At that point in his life he needs his teacher to be more concerned and more involved, not less. The student may misinterpret her actions as her not caring about him, which only leads to further deterioration of the student.

You can see this can become a vicious cycle. A cycle which is quite preventable by the teacher getting more training, but in particular, more experience in handling troubled kids. A little further on in this chapter, I will describe some ways in which teachers can get more training and experience so they too can join the team which wants to help keep small problems from becoming larger ones.

Put yourself in the teacher's skin for a moment. Let us suppose one day you are sitting at home and the doorbell rings. The man at the door says he is dropping off a foster kid for you to take care of over the next nine months. The man tells you this foster kid is a ten-year-old boy who has some behavioral problems like setting fires, stealing and running away from home. With that, the man leaves "the bundle on your doorstep" and departs. Probably the first thing you will feel like doing is chasing after the man and telling him to take this kid with him. But suppose you cannot catch him and you are stuck with the kid, then what? In other words, you suddenly find yourself faced with a task that you are poorly prepared for, and there are very few professional people around to help you with your new-found problem. You are going to be damned scared. You will probably try out a few things you already know about handling kids, but when they do not work you will get frustrated.

Perhaps you are getting an idea of how many teachers feel when they have kids who are not ready and eager to learn dropped on their doorsteps. The teachers are uncomfortable, scared and frustrated. And on top of all that, there are very few people in the school system that they can turn to for help. Remember how you chased after the man who dropped the kid on your doorstep? That is sometimes what teachers do when they are uncomfortable about a student. They send notes home to the parents or call them up on the phone or have conferences and say things like, "Make your kid learn." But if the teacher, who has been trained to teach this kid is unable to do it, how on earth are you, the parents going to make him learn? Certainly the parents must work with the teacher in solving the kid's problems, but the teacher cannot and should not get away with "passing the buck" back to the parents totally.

I regularly "get into it" with teachers because of this difference of opinion. I think largely teachers should be responsible to teach, and further, they need to be actively involved in finding out why a kid is unable or unwilling to learn. This business of calling up the parents and telling them to bring their kid back when he is ready to learn just does not work out very well. I think it is unwise, for the most part, for parents to get too involved with their kid's school work. As I said in Chapter XIV (School Problems), of course parents will be concerned and interested in how the kid is doing, but they should not get in the business of checking their kid's homework, forcing him to read for so many hours each night, or forcing him to learn.

It amazes me how I can sit and do play therapy with a five-year-old kid day in and day out for months, but completely lose my cool when I have to sit down and work with my own kids over their school work. And I am not that unusual. For most parents it becomes a tense, uncomfortable and totally unproductive situation when they start getting involved with their kid's school work. It is for the teacher to make the work interesting and exciting so the student will want to do it.

I am not that naive about teaching. I know that despite how magnificent the teachers demonstrations are, there are still going to be kids who have some emotional problems at home who express those problems by doing poorly in school. But it is the teacher's responsibility, particularly in those cases, to get involved with the parents and either help them herself or assist them in getting the help they need.

I would like to mention at this point two outstanding books that are absolutely essential reading for teachers. Doctor William Glasser is the author of both of these books and rather than trying to summarize his excellent observations and suggestions about teaching, I would rather ask that you, the teacher, read these two books. The first book is entitled *Reality Therapy* and the second is *Schools Without Failure*. They both are published by Harper and Row. Reading these two books will be an excellent first step in helping you, as the teacher, to deal with the anxiety and frustration you face concerning problem kids.

I would like to describe to you an experience I had a couple of years ago which I think will point out to you just how effective a genuinely concerned teacher can be. I was a consulting psychiatrist to several elementary schools and had the luxury of spending a fair amount of time actually within the confines of the school building. One day a first-grade school teacher, Miss Barbara Wright, came to me and said she would like to do something to help some of the kids she was teaching that year who exhibited severe behavioral problems. Her proposal sounded very interesting and, because we were both interested in children with behavioral problems, we set out to design an ideal program for these kids. Let me briefly describe that program to you.

Barbara was to be the teacher during a summer vacation and the program was called "The Behavior Modification Classroom" (BMC). We very carefully selected ten kids during the schoool year who were in kindergarten or first grade. All of these kids had been referred to the school counselor because of severe behavior problems. The parents of these kids were contacted, and they agreed to not only have their kid participate in this summer program, but agreed to be involved themselves in weekly sessions.

My role in this whole thing was probably the easiest of all. I met with Barbara for three hours each week and gave her moral support and encouragement, suggestions for dealing with the kids in the classroom situation and some advice as to how to go about working with the parents of these kids.

The kids came to Barbara's classroom each morning, Monday through Thursday, from 8:30 till 12:30, for a period of eight weeks.

They spent much of their day in the classroom and only occasionally took some field trips outside of the school building. They brought their lunches each day, and class was dismissed after lunch. Because none of these kids had academic problems, the overriding emphasis of the classroom was on behavior and socialization, not academics.

Each Friday morning Barbara would get together in a group lasting about an hour and one half with all the parents. There were several purposes of the parents' group. First of all, it was very helpful for these parents to see that there were other parents who faced many of the same problems they did and these couples were mutually supportive. Barbara was able to try out many behavior modification techniques in her working with the kids in the classroom and shared her successes and her failures with the parents. Likewise, the parents tried new techniques at home and shared their results weekly with Barbara and the rest of the group. The group used *Rules For Raising Kids* as a basis for working with the kids both at home and in the classroom.

It would be very hard to describe all of Barbara's techniques in the classroom. She was a calm but firm classroom teacher who rarely over-reacted and was generally unshakable. She employed many standard classroom techniques such as consistency and repetition, but emphasized certain other techniques that are less commonly employed. Much of the work in the classroom was based on Doctor Glasser's techniques as well as on the concept I have already described to you in Rule 3, the concept of reinforcement. In essence she rewarded good behavior and ignored bad behavior as much as it was safely possible to do so. When a student's behavior could no longer be ignored, then the quiet room (QR) was employed. I will describe the use of the QR in more detail in a moment.

The BMC went on as planned. At the end of the eight-week program Barbara wrote an evaluation on each of the kids. The parents too wrote an evaluation on the changes they had seen in their kids over that period of time, as well as what they themselves had learned in their weekly group sessions. Barbara followed up on the BMC by talking with the counselor and teachers of the ten kids during the course of the following school year. I must say honestly, the results were quite amazing. There was improvement in the behavior of every one of the kids in the program throughout the summer as judged by both the teacher and the parents. The parents felt they had resolved many of their family problems, particularly those problems centered around the kid who was in the BMC. They unanimously felt they learned new ways of coping with their kids' problems and in short felt they were well on their way to being successful parents. With every one of the kids in the BMC, the behavioral gains that were made by the end of the summer continued on during the school year with the new teacher, and we felt they were well on their way to becoming ingrained habits of good behavior.

What was so fascinating to me about this whole program, and the reason I am describing it to you here in detail, was that Barbara had never received any special training or experience in working with behaviorally disturbed kids other than her regular classroom experience. With the exception of my seeing only the parents on the very first interview during the school year, these families had no other contact with mental health professionals, "headshrinkers," school psychologists or school counselors. I lent some moral support as well as suggestions to the program, but essentially the program was carried on with great success by one teacher *who cared*. The most important ingredient in helping kids and troubled families is that you just need to "care." You do not have to have a PhD in clinical psychology and you do not have to be, as some teachers say, a "shrink" in the classroom; you just have to care. You have to get involved with your students and if need be, with the parents of your students. You do not have to "therapize" them, you just have to talk to them. If the teacher and parents will only just start talking, there is an excellent chance you will find some really very simple solutions.

Let me now describe to you the use of the QR in a little more detail. Barbara's classroom measured approximately forty feet by twenty feet. At one end of the room was the door and we placed our QR at the opposite end of the room because it was secluded.

This "elaborate" quiet room was built at a cost of ten dollars and consisted of two, four by eight foot sheets of ¼ inch plywood, fastened together at right angles and placed in the corner so as to set aside a small room. There was no door on the QR and one entered it through a one foot space between the plywood board and the wall. Inside the room was only one small chair facing the wall, no windows and nothing on the walls.

I would like to clear up one commonly held misconception before I go any further. It is not at all dangerous to isolate kids, providing there are certain minimal conditions. The isolation space should be a mini-

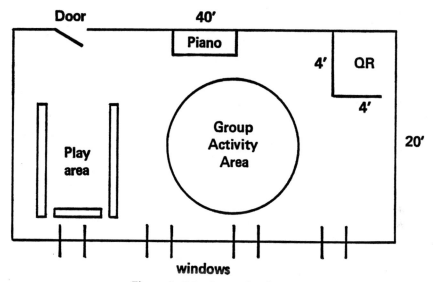

Figure 7. Schoolroom showing QR.

mum of four by four feet and at least six to eight feet high. There should be adequate lighting and ventilation. There should be nothing in the room except one chair, nothing on the walls and no windows to look out; that would only be a source of distraction. If the QR is adequately constructed and used wisely you need not be concerned about those old wives' tales about kids getting "stir-crazy."

What is most important about the QR is the way in which it is used. It should only be used when the kid's behavior in the classroom can no longer be ignored. The kids are told before hand what the QR is for and how it will be used. Certainly for many kids, it just arouses their suspicions and their testing nature, and they will need to find out first hand. When a kid's behavior can no longer be ignored or he is, for example, out of control, he is asked to go sit in the QR until he thinks he can control himself and then he can return to the rest of the class. He does not have to ask the teacher if he can come back, but he can come back on his own when he feels he is "in control." Many teachers wonder how you know when the kid is ready to come out. That is very easy. When he comes out and still is acting out of control, you point your finger toward the QR and back he goes. Frequently with a little experience you can tell just by the look on his face whether he is ready to come out and join the class. If he comes strutting out with that "I'll-be-damned-if-I'll-settle-down look," he is obviously not ready, and back he goes. You must be very careful in these situations to give the kid as little attention as possible while sending him to the QR. Frequently just a look and a point will be enough. Of course there may be times when you need to tell the kid specifically what behavior you are unhappy about, but generally kids know what they are being sent for, and after the QR has been in use for just a little while, they will know when they are in control enough to come back.

This is really an excellent technique to use for kids with behavioral problems, particularly if much of the bad behavior is for attention getting reasons. The QR is particularly successful with kids from ages three to thirteen. There is one kind of kid, however, who probably should not be placed in the QR. He is the one who daydreams or fantasizes a great deal and in fact sometimes gets lost in his fantasies. If he were placed in a QR, that probably would be quite a reward for him, since he would be able to get away from the classroom noise which had been disturbing his daydreams. This kind of kid though will almost never need a QR because his behavior is usually not disruptive or attention getting.

I have had a lot of experience with QR's over the years in a variety of settings ranging from working with severely disturbed kids in children's psychiatric hospitals, using them in schools and principles' offices, as well as having parents construct them in the home. It has not very often been necessary to have parents construct a QR in the home, but I remember well some very important successes I have had with them. I remember one father who built an elaborate quiet room in one of the bedrooms in his home. His seven-year-old son (who was to be the chief occupant of the QR) very carefully watched his father work for several days at the project. As Dad built it he very carefully explained to his son the purpose of the QR and how it was to be used. What was so interesting was that once the QR was finished, the kid never once needed to use it. You could not ask for a better result than that.

As you can tell, I believe in the QR. Whether at home or in the classroom, a kid who does not have good "internal" control needs to have "external" control provided for him. The QR is an excellent way to provide this external control.

Again let me say the teacher is the first line of defense in the classroom. She must be, in essence, the mental health consultant for all the kids in her class. Let us be honest and face facts. There are not enough counselors, school psychologists, social workers and psychiatrists to even scratch the surface. Nor will there ever be enough. But the solution to the problem of helping kids learn does not lie in training more psychiatrists. The solution lies in helping teachers see their role for what it is; the person who must, on a daily basis, look at and work with the total kid, his academic performance, his behavior, his feelings and when need be, his family.

Certainly there are going to be other professionals around to help the teacher with her task, but their role can and should be a minor one. They will be called in only in those cases that are too complex or difficult for the teacher to handle. After all I am not saying the teacher should be a psychologist or a psychiatrist. What I am saying is that *a caring, competent teacher can handle the majority of problems that come along.* The problems she cannot handle can be referred to the counselor or psychologist.

There are other services in the community that may be called upon when needed, for instance, the child psychiatrist, the inpatient psychiatric facility, the pediatrician, the juvenile court and the family service agency, just to name a few.

I would estimate that about fifty percent of all school children, either because of limited IQ, learning disabilities or emotional factors, are not fully *able* to learn. But teachers who care and are willing to get involved can significantly help that fifty percent be ready and able to learn.

Such a system as I have described, if working properly, benefits everyone in the community. The kid is happier because he has help with his problem and he is doing better in school, and he is getting along better with his family. The parents are happier because they have gotten some help with their problem kid and what is more, they have gotten it early and at a price that will not cause them to go into bankruptcy. The teacher is happier, because she is now able to teach since she has kids who are able to learn. The icing on the cake for the teacher is that she can feel a real sense of pride and accomplishment at doing more than just teaching the three R's. Certainly the entire community benefits because its "problem children" have gotten help early, when they need it, when the problems are small. The teacher and the school have assisted the family in preventing those small problems from becoming large ones.

CHAPTER XVII

Bed-Wetting and Soiling

Hopefully as adults we communicate a large part of our feelings by using words, and we can call this verbal communication. If a guy is angry at his wife because she dented the fender of their car, he probably hollers at her or at least raises his voice and says something like, "I wish you'd keep your hands off my car." He probably, at the same time though, is sending her some nonverbal messages also. The angry look he has on his face is certainly a message to his wife, and his angrily waving his fists in the air is certainly another nonverbal message. These obvious verbal and nonverbal messages we all tend to pick up for the most part, but it is the more subtle ones we sometimes overlook and by our overlooking these subtle messages, we frequently get into trouble.

Let us suppose you are over at a friend's house some evening, and you are sitting around talking, and it is getting quite late. Your host is probably giving you some subtle nonverbal messages, perhaps by yawning or rubbing his eyes, that he is tired and he wants you to go home. But because you are overlooking those messages, you stay on for another couple of hours. He finally practically has to throw you out of the house, and he probably will never invite you back again.

Actually this is truly a two part problem; first of all, his messages are not direct enough (perhaps he could say he is getting tired). The second part of the problem is you do not pick up on the subtle messages he is sending.

Kid's messages are even more difficult to figure out. They rarely give us verbal messages. For example, little babies, because they have not obtained talking skills, cry when they are hungry. They do not say, "Hey, Mom, pass the bottle." Hopefully as they get older they get a little better at telling us verbally, particularly if we encourage them.

Mostly kids tell us things by behavior and then we are left with the tough job of figuring out what the behavior means and then trying to respond to it. Where we get into trouble is that we forget *behavior represents a message*. If we just look at it as behavior, that does not help us at all. For example, if you look at a yawn as just a yawn, it will have little meaning to you. But if you think of it as a message or a way another person is trying to communicate with you, it is fairly easy to figure out the meaning and then to do something about it. Another example we have already talked about is the temper tantrum. If you look at that just as bad behavior, you probably will not know how to deal with it correctly. But it you look at it as a message the kid is trying to send you, very quickly you realize he is showing his anger, but he is mostly trying to get attention from you. Of course you would then ignore it.

What does all this have to do with a kid wetting his bed or soiling his pants? The answer is simple. These too are messages kids are sending us, but messages that all too often fall on our deaf ears. If we look at the behavior as just bed-wetting and soiling, we are probably not going to get anywhere. If we look at it as the kid's trying to tell us something through his behavior, we will have a much better chance of figuring out what he is trying to say, and then what we should do about it.

Let me clear up one common misconception. About 85 percent of the kids who wet the bed, do it for emotional reasons. Another 10 percent do it because they sleep too soundly and another 5 percent do it for other physical reasons. Let us take a look now at the 5 percent who do it for physical reasons.

I have no intention of giving you a basic course in urology or listing all the thousand and one physical causes for bed-wetting, but just a few examples will give you some ideas of what I am talking about. Probably some of the most common physical causes for bed-wetting are such things as urinary tract infections (bladder/or kidneys), or when parts of the urinary system have not formed properly. Girls of all ages, but particularly three to five-year-old girls, love to stick things into their vaginas because it feels good. But because the opening to the bladder is so close to the opening of the vagina, this practice very frequently results in bladder infections in little girls. Sometimes after a bowel movement little girls will wipe themselves by moving the tissue forward instead of backward, therefore dragging the soiled toilet paper right across the vagina and opening to the bladder, which is also a common source of infection. But for whatever reason the infection gets started, one of the first signs of a urinary tract infection is that kids will have to pee very frequently, and because they are not used to having to pee frequently, they sometimes will lose it in their pants before getting into the bathroom. Or they will not wake up at night and they will wet the bed. It is rare for a little kid to go to her Mommy and say, "Mommy, I have to pee frequently." In other words they do not tell you verbally, but they will tell you nonverbally by their behavior, either by wetting themselves during the day or by wetting the bed at night.

Even though we are dealing with a very small percentage (5%) of all bed-wetters, it is certainly an essential part of looking into why your kid wets the bed, to take him to your family doctor and ask him for his opinion. Very frequently just a history, a physical examination, and a urine test will be sufficient to rule out physical causes of bed-wetting. However, many physicians feel a special kidney X-ray, an IVP, is indicated whenever there is a long-standing problem with bed-wetting. These tests and examinations are very easily accomplished and in a few weeks you will know whether there is any physical reason for the bed-wetting. If there is a physical reason, of course, then your physician will treat that condition and that will be the end of that.

The other ten percent of bed-wetters I referred to, the sound sleepers, have only been discovered in recent years. Many parents have always said their kids wet the bed because they just sleep too deeply. In recent years, because of advances in brain wave studies, doctors have been able to test kids to find out just how deeply they sleep. And in fact, they can tell by the brain wave tracings very clearly that there are four stages or four depths of sleep. They have called these stages one, two, three and four. In the studies that have been done they have actually observed kids who, while hooked up to the brain wave machine, have been sleeping and have wet the bed during the test. They have found from these studies that some kids spend a great deal of time in the fourth or deepest stage of sleep and only wet themselves when they are in that fourth stage.

Let us suppose you are an average person and you happen to have a beer or two just before going to sleep. After about two hours your bladder fills up and becomes quite distended. This sends an impulse from your bladder up to your brain which wakes up your brain and tells you to "get into the bathroom" before you lose something. You very quickly wake up, stagger into the "john," relieve yourself and go back to bed. In the kids who sleep too soundly, their bladder fills up, sends a message up to their brain, but their brain is so sound asleep it does not hear the message. It is like the bladder knocking on the door of the brain but nobody is home. The kid has no alternative but to wet the bed.

How do you make this diagnosis? I have found usually just by questioning the parents we can decide whether the kid is wetting because he sleeps too soundly or whether it is due to an emotional problem. Parents of these kids will tell you the kid plays hard all day and frequently, when he goes to sleep, collapses into bed and goes into a very sound sleep. They will further tell you that you can practically take the bed out from under him and he will not wake up. He sleeps through noises and turning on the light and other sorts of things that would ordinarily wake a kid up. Only a few places in the United States go as far to do brain wave tests on these kids. It is probably much simpler just to try the kid on medication if you suspect he is wetting because he is a sound sleeper. The medications most commonly used are the antidepressants, specifically Tofranil®, Elavil®, or Aventyl®. It probably is not because this has anything to do with depression, it was just accidentally discovered these medicines seem to help. They probably help because they tend to keep the kid from going into the very deepest stages of sleep, so that when his bladder does send a message up to his brain, his brain will be in a shallow enough stage of sleep that it can wake up.

If you are going to progress in a step-wise fashion in trying to understand and help your kid with his bed-wetting, the first place to start is with your family doctor. He can, first of all, make sure there are no physical reasons for the bed-wetting. The second thing he can do, particularly if you and the doctor think the wetting might be caused by your kid's sleeping too soundly, is to try medication. These medicines are quite safe in the correct dose and you have very little to lose in trying them.

The third category, by far the largest (85% of bed-wetters), is made up of kids who wet the bed for emotional reasons. It is with this group in particular that we must be very careful to look at the behavior as a message, and then to try to figure out what the message means and how to respond to it. The two most common messages hidden in the behavior of bed-wetting are, "Piss on you" and "You're scaring the piss out of me." In the first message there is no question this is a very angry message. This perhaps is a kid whose parents are riding him about his bed-wetting, but most commonly they are on him about something else. Perhaps, as in Rule 1, the parents are fighting a lot of battles they cannot win and this is the kid's way of show-ing them what he thinks about that! Another example might be the family which is having some problems with Rule 4, the kid is trying to get back at them, but since he cannot do it directly, he is doing it indirectly by wetting the bed.

Remember in the chapter on discipline I talked about how spank-ing and how other kinds of overreaction on the part of the parents can be frightening to kids. Bed-wetting may be how your kid is tell-ing you he is frightened.

Bed-wetting may also point to other kinds of fears. Several years ago I received notice there was a good chance I would be drafted and sent to Viet Nam. I discussed this openly with all the members of my family since I felt it best to prepare them for the possibility of that happening. My kids surprised me because they, at least overtly, did not seem to react much to that. But over the next few weeks one of my daughters began having some trouble in school, began sucking her thumb and also started wetting the bed. I took her aside on sev-eral occasions to try to get her to express some of her feelings to me verbally instead of nonverbally and after a while she finally broke down and started crying. She was finally able to *tell* me she was scared I would be sent to Viet Nam and I would get killed and never come back. I tried to reassure her it was not very likely that would happen, but since I was just as scared myself, my reassurance did not help very much. A few days later I got my induction notice and my orders to Germany, which I promptly shared with the rest of my family. From that day on, the bed-wetting disappeared and has never returned. In other words, her bed-wetting represented a message, "Daddy, I am scared you will get killed." Once I was able to understand the mes-sage, then I could respond to it appropriately.

There are many frightening things in kids' lives which they try to tell us about by wetting the bed. As I have mentioned earlier, kids have sexy ideas at ages much younger than we realize. They may not really understand about intercourse at age four, but they certainly recognize the sexy feeling they get when, for example, little boys see their mothers undress. Sometimes situations that are too sexually stimulating become scary, resulting in bed-wetting. I saw a case re-cently that nicely demonstrates the point. This was a family where there was a boy age four and a girl aged six. Dad was a salesman and was on the road a great deal. Little Teddy would frequently wake up at night crying because he was having a scary dream. These almost always occurred when Dad was gone. Mom found what she thought was a simple solution by taking Teddy to bed with her so he would sleep through the night. Also Mom had a habit of not being careful about modesty and the kids were free to come in and out of the bathroom when she was taking a bath. It was not very long after this, that Teddy started wetting the bed pretty regularly. On the first visit I had with this family we were able to see that perhaps this was an uncomfortable or even scary situation for Teddy. It was almost as if Teddy was too stimulated by his having Mom all to himself in bed and seeing her undressed occasionally. He was probably further scared by feeling that Dad might come home and find out he had some sexual feelings about Mom. The solution in this case was very simple. Mom began insisting on Teddy's sleeping in his own room and she also began to be more careful about keeping the bathroom door closed when she was bathing, and keeping her bedroom door closed when she was dressing. A few days after that, the bed-wetting ceased and never again returned.

It is for this reason that I encourage parents to establish some pretty firm rules in their homes about people sleeping in their own bed. It is also a good idea to be careful about modesty, particularly after the kids are aged two or three. These simple precautions will frequently prevent overstimulation and prevent the kids from becoming overly fearful.

You can see that if a kid is wetting the bed, most commonly the reasons will be emotional ones. It is a good idea then to study the eight basic rules very carefully and see if and where you are making some mistakes in raising the kids. I am always troubled when I hear parents say, "Oh, it's just a stage he is going through and he'll probably outgrow it." I see many families who take this approach and therefore never really get to the basic causes of the problem. All too often their kids will not only go on wetting the bed for many, many years, but also will frequently develop behavioral problems in other areas as well.

A similar approach can be successfully used in trying to help kids who soil their pants during the day or soil themselves when they are asleep. Again, frequently the messages are the same, "Crap on you" or "You're scaring the crap out of me." Again it is always essential to start by seeing your family doctor to rule out any physical causes for the soiling, but most frequently you will find that the soiling represents a message. The kid is trying to tell you that something is going on in his life he is unhappy about or that is scaring him. Once you understand the message you will have little difficulty in knowing what to do about it.

In these cases, not only does punishment never work, but it usually makes the problem worse. Spankings, scoldings or putting the kid down ("only babies do that") will only cause the kid to become even more angry and probably wet or soil even more frequently. You must find out what you are doing to make him angry or scared, and then stop it. Fighting battles over this area (that you certainly cannot win), will only make it worse. Once you have corrected what you were doing wrong, you should say to the kid, "I know accidents happen, so if you happen to wet the bed some night, that's okay. Just pull down the covers when you do wet the bed so the bed can dry out." In other words, tell him exactly what you would like to do about it, but avoid having him bring it to your attention. Also it is a good idea not to go in and check his bed to see if he has had an accident, because this will only draw more attention to the problem and will probably make it worse.

Some physicians feel that rewarding the kid for not wetting or soiling is a good idea, but in my experience, this rarely works, and I would encourage you not to use that approach. For instance, some people would suggest giving the kid a nickel for each night he does not wet the bed or keeping a chart and giving him a star for every night he does not wet. These techniques just draw more attention to the problem and make a big deal out of it. The approach that will work most frequently will be to ignore it completely and leave it up to him. Do not ignore your part in the problem, you need to correct that; but make it *his* responsibility, when an accident happens, he can handle it on his own.

Frequently kids will hide their underwear when they make a mess in it or try to cover up a wet bed in the morning. But they will only do that if they are scared you will be angry with them or if you have made them ashamed for doing that. Almost always the problem will correct itself if you stop the battles that are going on concerning the wetting or soiling and stop "playing games" over it.

If you are one of those fortunate ones who still have not begun potty training, I can give you some advice which may help you very much. If you are busy scrubbing diapers every week, you probably do not think you are fortunate, but I really mean fortunate in a different sense. You have the whole area of potty training ahead of you which can be a very simple thing to go through with your kid, or it can be a disaster, depending on how you handle it. You are fortunate because you have the opportunity to prevent him from ever having a problem with bed-wetting, soiling, and stubbornness.

You are probably wondering what stubbornness has to do with bed-wetting, but I think they are very much related. The whole business of going in the potty is really your kid's first chance in life to assert his independence, for him to completely have his own way. Remember I said in Rule 1, potty is a battle you cannot win and should not fight. That means no matter what you do, your kid is going to become potty trained when he wants to and when he is good and ready, so accept this as a fact. Admit to yourself there is nothing you can do about it, so you are going to handle it very cautiously and comfortably for the both of you and not create any hard feelings over it. If you take the other approach, namely that you are going to fight with him and you are going to be the boss over when he goes in the potty, you are going to lose and what is more, you are going to create a lot of hard feelings between you and your kid. You will be taking the first step in making him one stubborn kid for the rest of his life.

If you can accept the fact that he is going to be the boss, the whole business of potty training is really very simple. You should wait until he is about two to three years of age. You should buy him a little potty chair of his very own, something small that he can drag around the house and use as a regular chair for a little while. I think preferably it should have arms and it should be a comfortable little chair, because after all you want him to become fond of it. Let him drag it around the house and sit on it and enjoy it as his "special chair." After a few weeks of this you start sitting him on it a couple of times a day without his pants on and you might even try sprinkling a little warm water over his penis which frequently gives kids the idea to start peeing. If you are patient, sooner or later, probably by accident, he will do a job in the potty. At that point you will become very excited and smile and tell him how pleased you are, and "gush all over him." He will be so happy you are pleased, he will want to do it again for all that reward. Of course, he is going to continue using his diaper as well for a while, but as time goes by he will, with increasing frequency, start going in the potty. Because he is doing nothing wrong you certainly would not want to scold him for going in his diapers, however, you are just going to leave that up to him.

A lot of mothers have the misconception that they want to get their kid potty trained early so they can get him out of diapers and they can save themselves the drudgery of that laundry problem every week. But it most frequently does not work out that way. If you start trying to potty train too early and take a kid out of diapers, he just will not be ready and he will do his business every place else instead of in the potty. Now which would you rather do? Wash a few diapers every week or wash everything from his training pants, trousers, shoes and socks, to the sheets and blankets, and even the living room carpeting? The ideal situation is just to simply wait until he is ready and for most kids this is sometime between the age of two and three. If you use this positive approach, not only will he develop good potty habits, but he will be well on his way to developing a healthy personality because he will learn there are certain areas of his life in which he can assert himself and do what he wants. Potty is one of those areas in which kids need to assert their independence.

CHAPTER XVIII

Eating Problems

If your children are young, you still have the opportunity of avoiding eating problems. As you recall, eating too is one of those battles you cannot win and therefore you must not fight. It is also a major area where your kid can assert his independence, his initiative and his freedom of choice. If you stifle that by demanding he eat certain things, not only will you lose the eating battle, but you will be well on your way to making his stubbornness much worse.

Eating is one thing in our society that gets blown way out of proportion. Just leaf through a magazine and see for yourself how food ads dominate all others. Or watch television for a few hours and see the overabundance of food commercials. We have become preoccupied with eating to the point where being overweight is a major health problem in the United States today. After housing, eating probably represents the biggest expense in our budgets.

Very simply, the point I am trying to make is Americans have a "thing" about eating. That is not important until you recall what I said earlier about how when kids want to get back at us, they get us "where we live." Well, for many of us "where we live" is our stomach. When kids want to get back at us indirectly, they do it in areas we are sensitive about. For instance, what could get to Mom more than Junior's refusing to eat anything, after she has spent hours in the kitchen preparing a nice meal? Or after Dad has gone out and worked hard for the money to have food on the table, for the kids to turn their noses up at it?

Suppose your kid came to you and said, "Oh, your grandmother has a moustache." You would probably laugh it off and that would be that. You are not sensitive about your grandmother having a moustache. But when your kid comes to you and says, "I hate vegetables and I do not want to eat them," that really gets to you because of the way you have been raised. In a way, you have been brainwashed into being sensitive about eating. For example, you have been taught that spinach is good for kids, but is it? Not in particular. It has about the same food value as grass with a few vitamins thrown in. That is true of most vegetables. And how about milk? We have

135

all been taught milk is next to cleanliness and godliness. But is it really essential that kids drink that much milk?

There were some interesting studies done during the Korean War that will make you question whether you want to force your kid to drink milk. The Army did autopsies for several years on every man killed between the ages of eighteen and twenty-one. What they found on these grown-up "milk-fed babies" was that, almost without exception, every young GI autopsied had evidence of hardening of the arteries. That statistic absolutely shocked physicians all over the world. Here were young, supposedly healthy, Americans who died of battle injuries, and who showed evidence of heart disease and hardening of the arteries at such a tender age. Arteries like that come from the way we Americans eat and also probably from our lack of exercise.

There are other interesting statistics that will point out to you what our overeating is doing to us. We have one of the highest rates of heart attack of any people in the world. Why? Many physicians think it is almost entirely due to our diet which is high in milk, fats, and cholesterol. Do you know that in all the years the concentration camps were going during the Second World War, there was never a heart attack reported in a prisoner? You just do not get heart attacks if you do not eat rich, fat foods like milk and fatty meats and eggs. In the poor, black communities in the rural South, heart attacks are almost nonexistent for the same reason.

It is bad enough that *we* are eating ourselves to death; do we have to teach our kids to do that too? And yet we do it all the time. We demand that our kids eat their vegetables, drink their milk, and we fight a lot of battles, and we play a lot of games with them. And as that old expression goes, "We can't win for losing," but we do it.

I have seen two cases in which girls died because they got into such severe battles over eating with their mothers. Of course that is quite an extreme for stubbornness to go to, but the point is, if your kid does not really want to eat, she is not going to, despite anything you might try to do. In the cases of the two girls, the surgeons even went as far as to put tubes into their stomachs so they could be fed directly into the stomach, but that did not help because they just vomited the food right back up. Intravenous feedings did not work either and the two girls just died.

Another one of our misconceptions is that you have to eat a lot to be strong and healthy and to keep your mind going. Yet people who have lived to be 105 have eaten tiny quantities of food every day of their lives and still remained healthy. You do need a fairly well-balanced diet to stay healthy, but after all your body will get that if it has a choice. What I am saying is you do not need a very large quantity of food, probably a whole lot less than most of us realize. Did you know your brain can run effectively for a period of twenty-four hours from the energy stored in one peanut? And yet how many of us demand that our kids have a good breakfast in the morning so they can think well in school?

Let us suppose you have an infant at home still on the bottle and strained food. Your job is pretty simple from the time the kid is born till he is about one to one and a half. You are going to give him pretty much what your doctor recommends; you will offer him his bottle several times a day, and as he gets older you will introduce a fairly well-balanced diet of strained foods and junior foods. (It is probably a good idea to offer him the foods before his bottle because it seems as though some kids just want to live on the bottle completely and never even try other foods.)

Most of us do pretty well up to that point. It is when the kid starts on table food that we start getting up tight. And really, there is no need for that at all. At mealtime Mom should call the family to the table. The television should go off because that just interrupts people in the family from talking to one another at the table. In our busy society, mealtime is one of the few times we have an opportunity to talk to each other. Mom can either dish up the food into plates or just put the food on the table in serving dishes and let the family help themselves. Remember that study I mentioned earlier about how rats and kids will get exactly what their bodies need? If you put the food on the table the kids will help themselves to what their bodies need, no more, no less. Isn't that really what you want them to do? If they do it this way they will never get too skinny or too fat, and they will never be deficient in vitamins or minerals. If mom never puts anything on the table that contains vitamin B_{12}, there is a good chance the kid is going to be deficient in B_{12}. But that is practically impossible to do nowadays, with vitamin supplements in milk, bread, cereal and many of the other things we eat every day. I am not at all saying mom can just throw any old junk on the table. Hopefully she is going to continue to cook nice, appetizing, well-balanced meals the family will want to eat.

Because dessert is part of the meal the kid gets dessert if he wants it. He does not have to pass any tests like eating a certain number of peas or drinking so much of his milk to get his dessert. If he wants to have two helpings of mashed potatoes and no green vegetables, that is fine too. Evidently his body does not need vegetables right then.

There are a couple of exceptions to this free eating policy I would like to mention now. Because most of us are not wealthy and cannot afford an unlimited supply of food, no one kid is allowed to eat other people's portions. If there are four people in your family and you put enough mashed potatoes in the bowl for one serving per person, it would be unfair for one kid to eat more than his share.

Also keep in mind that I am not talking about kids' having the freedom to do what they want to do at the table. You are still going to expect reasonably good manners at the table and you are going to expect the kids to sit there until most of the family is finished and Mom or Dad excuses them. A kid's flinging mashed potatoes or a napkin across the table would call for his being excused to go to his room until he thinks he can come back to the table without having to do that.

There is the question of between meal snacks. How many of us adults really need to eat between meals? For most of us that is one of our biggest sources of being overweight. It is important for us to set a good example for the kids by not having a lot of food lying around in between meals (dishes of candy or bowls of potato chips and dip in the evenings). That is just totally unnecessary and worst of all it encourages the kids to eat between meals because that places a coating of sugar on their teeth for most of their waking hours and just invites cavities and other dental problems. Further, if a kid eats between meals he is not going to be hungry at mealtime and he probably will not feel like eating the nourishing food Mom has prepared for him.

Suppose you find while you are reading this, or perhaps have recognized it earlier, that you and your family are fighting a lot of battles over eating. Keep in mind how kids "fight dirty." You may be demanding they eat certain things and they may seem to be going along with you. But does that really mean they are not fighting back? Of course not. I have seen many families in this situation where the kids are smart enough not to fight back directly over the food. They just go ahead and eat what they are told, but they fight back by doing poorly in school or by behaving badly at home.

What do you do if you find you have an eating problem in your family? Again a good place to start is with your family doctor. He can examine your kid and perhaps run a few simple tests and know very quickly if there is any physical problem getting in the way of his eating. For example, a kid with an underactive thyroid gland will seem as though he does not have much appetite, but that everything he eats "turns to fat." But physical or medical problems account for a very small percentage of eating problems. Mostly kids have eating problems because there is something emotional going on between parents and kid.

A few years ago a man brought his twelve-year-old son in to see me with the initial complaint that, "My son hasn't eaten a vegetable in eight years." I thought at first that perhaps Dad was exaggerating, but in fact he was not. For most of this boy's life, Dad had been demanding that his son eat vegetables, and of course his son was refusing. Dad tried forcing the food down his throat, he tried restrictions to the house, he tried rewards and punishments, and he tried spanking. But no matter what he tried, the problem was still the same, his son would not eat vegetables.

I explained to the father about my philosophy and why kids need to have a choice in what they eat. I further suggested he go home and say, "Look, Carl, this is ridiculous. We have been fighting over vegetables for eight years now until you are miserable and I am miserable. From now on there are going to be no more fights over food. You are just going to eat what you want to eat. You are going to come to the table when Mom calls and if you want to sit there and eat nothing, that is all right too. But most important, you eat whatever you want to of the things that Mom puts on the table."

I also reminded Dad that his son was going to have to test him. He would probably still go on for a few more meals eating a pretty unbalanced diet, or perhaps that he might not eat anything at the next meal.

The next evening I was sitting at home reading the paper and I got a phone call from this man. He was so excited he practically screamed to me over the phone, "My kid has eaten a vegetable for the first time in eight years." That really surprised the father, but it was no surprise to me. I know kids will really make excellent decisions, if the decisions are truly left up to them. Nowhere is this more evident than with the problem of eating.

You are probably sitting there trying to think up some excuse for why this approach should not be used with your kid. You are probably thinking, "Well, he's too fat and if I let him eat all he wants, he'll just get even fatter." Or perhaps you are thinking, "It's only my demanding that he eats that keeps him from starving to death." Nonsense. If you have a fat kid or a skinny kid and there have been no major physical problems, it is probably because you have been butting your nose in far too long. If you are offended or you are sore at me, that is really unimportant. What is important is that you sit down and talk to your kid and tell him you are going to butt out of his eating. If he is overweight and he wants to go on a diet, he probably knows, or you can tell him *once,* what foods are high in calories and what foods are low in calories, and you might even suggest you buy a little book about it, but from then on it should be up to him.

As parents our obligation is to put a well-balanced meal on the table. After that it is up to the kids.

CHAPTER XIX

The Overactive Kid

This chapter is not just about the kid who is overactive, but it is really about a very special kind of overactive kid we call by many names. He may be called the hyperactive child or he may be said to have the *hyperkinetic syndrome*. A syndrome is a collection of symptoms that fall together nicely under one heading. For example, the "flu" syndrome consists of a number of symptoms such as headache, weakness, nausea, vomiting and diarrhea. The hyperkinetic syndrome is also a collection of symptoms. Only one of the symptoms in this syndrome is overactivity and, as you will see, there are many other symptoms that go along with it.

Let me make it clear that kids can be overactive for mainly three different reasons. The first one, and the one we are primarily discussing in this chapter, is the child who is overactive because his brain is not working quite right to slow him down. This is the hyperkinetic syndrome.

The second category of overactive kid is the one who is raised in a very tense family situation. As you probably have experienced, tension is contagious. All you need to do is sit around a married couple who is having a spat and pretty soon you will start feeling tense yourself. This is the way it is with the kid who is raised in a tense family and he shows his tension frequently in overactivity.

It is sometimes difficult to distinguish whether a kid is overactive because he is hyperkinetic or whether he is overactive because he comes from a tense family. This task is made easier if you will keep in mind that the hyperkinetic kid is overactive from birth, whereas the tense kid does not really start getting overactive until about age four to six.

The third category is the severely disturbed child who is suffering from schizophenia or infantile autism. Fortunately these conditions are very rare and a kid with one of these conditions shows behavior quite different from the other two groups I have mentioned above. It is also important to note that *only* the hyperkinetic kid possesses most of the following symptoms.

Let me now describe to you some of the features or symptoms of the hyperkinetic syndrome. The overactivity in this syndrome is a continuous activity. Most of us are overactive at some time in our lives, but this child has his motor running overtime. It seems as though he never stops from morning till night, when he finally collapses into bed. He cannot sit still; he fidgets and is disruptive in the classroom. He almost always has a very short attention span. All of us have a hard time concentrating on things that bore us, but this child cannot even concentrate for very long on things that are interesting to him, like a favorite television program. His mind (and frequently, his body) just keeps jumping from one topic to another. He is easily distracted, he is frequently aggressive, and he has a hard time adjusting to new situations. He may be overly irritable and it may seem that almost anything will set him off. He has a hard time waiting for things and seems to be a very needy kid. He is impulsive and thinks he should do whatever pops into his head. He frequently for that reason is accident prone, and may be generally clumsy as well. Although he is of normal intelligence, he often has difficulty in school, especially in math, reading and writing.

You must keep in mind a hyperkinetic kid does not have to have all of the symptoms mentioned above. Most often he will have the overactivity and the short attention span as well as a few of the other things mentioned. If this is starting to sound a little bit like the "little monster" you have at home, do not feel alone about your frustration with him. Most parents have a very hard time tolerating their hyperkinetic kids.

The hyperkinetic kid is not usually discovered until the kid gets to kindergarten or first grade because his inability to sit still does not show up very much as long as he has the kind of freedom he has at home. But just try to make him sit still in a classroom for three hours and you and the teacher have trouble on your hands. The hyperkinetic kid is frequently noticeable right from the beginning. He may be overactive in the crib and may do other things like banging his head or rocking back and forth. Sometimes when mother picks him up he may be unusually stiff or even unusually flimsy. He often does a lot of things early, like crawling and walking, and certainly starts getting into things at a very early age. Even his emotional ups and downs are noticeable early, and frequently he has temper tantrums or does an unusual amount of crying. It seems right from the beginning this little fellow needs less sleep than other kids his age.

I would like to take a moment and explain what is behind this business of the hyperkinetic syndrome. If we simplify it, you can think of the brain as being composed of two parts. One part is like the gas pedal in your car. It is what makes you go and gives you all the drive. The other part is like the brakes in your car, which is in charge of self-control and of making you slow down and stop. Ordinarily, when a child is born, these two forces are in pretty good balance, that is, the go equals the stop. The hyperkinetic kid, however, has all the normal amount of drive, but his brakes are poor. If you were driving a car with a normal gas pedal and poor brakes, you would be constantly banging into things and getting into trouble, and that is exactly what happens to a hyperkinetic kid.

The hyperkinetic syndrome occurs much more commonly than most people realize. About 4 percent of the population of school age children suffer from this condition—about one million kids in the United States. It is slightly more common in first-born males. Many professionals feel this condition is passed along in families, whereas others feel it is one of those accidents of birth. There may have been some difficulty during the pregnancy or delivery or just after delivery, but for whatever reason, the brakes just do not work as well as the gas pedal.

How do you make the diagnosis of hyperkinetic syndrome? This is one of those instances in medicine where the parents and teachers do a much better job of diagnosing than the doctors. The reason for this is that the most helpful single thing in making the diagnosis is the history of the child's behavior, and who knows better than the parents and teacher. Brain wave tests (EEG) are frequently normal. Psychological tests are only occasionally of some value. Sometimes trying the kid on medication will help in the diagnosis; the child from a tense family situation gets worse on medication and the hyperkinetic child usually calms down. It is the kid's behavior that is the problem, and the people who observe his behavior usually are the best diagnosticians.

Over a period of several years I have had some interesting experiences by going into schools and asking the principals about the "worst kids you have in this school." Frequently the principals would rattle off several of their "favorites." I would then talk with these kids, talk to their parents and teachers, and in a large number of cases I would find out these were hyperkinetic kids who had never been diagnosed or treated. In other words, these were not bad kids, but they sure did get into a lot of trouble.

A moment ago I mentioned treating these kids with medicine. Probably, if we did nothing, almost all of these kids would outgrow the condition by the time they were teenagers. Then the question arises, why medicate? I can answer this question mainly in two ways. First of all, from the age of four to say twelve, kids are supposed to be learning the very basic fundamentals of education, what the teachers call building blocks. Without these basics, such as math, reading and writing, the kids would have a very difficult time later on in school. If the children are not treated during these years, they will likely have an extremely difficult time paying attention and learning in school and will miss out on a great deal of basic information. By treating them, they are able to sit still, concentrate, pay attention, and most important of all, learn.

The second important reason we like to treat kids with medication is that without medication they are frequently going to get into trouble. Like the example I gave before of your driving your car without brakes and getting into trouble, these kids will get into trouble socially. Because of their emotional outbursts, their overactivity, their aggressiveness and their fighting, they will start to develop some bad habits in getting along with people, not only people their own age, but especially adults. Even though they may outgrow the condition at age twelve, the bad habits are likely to continue for a lifetime. Therefore the second important reason for treating these children with medication is to *prevent* them from developing bad habits in getting along with people.

At first glance the treatment with medicine seems kind of strange, especially when you consider the kind of medicines we use. The medicines most commonly prescribed are the stimulants, Dexedrine® and Ritalin®. Why give kids stimulants who are already overly stimulated? The answer is simple. It is like putting power brakes on your car, if your brakes have not been working well. They help you to slow down and stop better. So it is in using stimulants with hyperkinetic kids. The stimulants act only on the "brake" part of their brain and stimulate the brakes to work better. They help the kids slow down, pay attention and concentrate; the medicines stimulate self-control.

At this point you are probably thinking, "That crazy shrink is trying to put my kid on dope." Laugh if you will, but many parents react this way and it is understandable why they do. Like any other medicine, whether it be aspirin or penicillin, the stimulants can and frequently are misused. We have all heard about the hippies injecting tremendous doses of stimulants into their veins to get high. But the doses we use are small and are quite safe. The stimulants have been used since 1938 to treat this condition, and there has *never* been a case of addiction or habituation reported. There are occasionally some nuisance side effects, such as the medicine's bothering the kids' appetites or their sleep. But usually, if given in the right dose at the right time, these side effects are extremely rare.

Probably the most important thing about this whole business is once the doctor starts a kid on medicine, particularly at the beginning, parents teachers and doctor must keep in fairly close contact. It is always the goal of the doctor to have the medicine work well on the smallest possible dose, and that will be up to the doctor, the parents, and the teacher to decide. Often I find the teacher is the best judge of the dose of medication because she sees the kid in the situation that is the most demanding for him, sitting still in the classroom. She also sees the child at the peak of the medicine's effectiveness, since it is given in the morning and at noon, and only lasts three to four hours.

The question always arises as to how long a child needs to be on medicine. The answer is really very simple—as long as it takes. Let us suppose your kid is started on medication and does well on it; by that I mean, he is less active, he is able to pay attention and learn better, and he gets into less trouble. He probably will need to be on it until his early teens. It certainly does not hurt to try the child without the medicine, but you should keep in mind the time to stop the medicine is when the child's own self-control (brakes) has developed sufficiently. At that point he should be able to slow down without medicine.

I generally encourage parents to give their kid the medicine on the weekends and during the summer vacation. The reason is that important learning goes on during weekends and summertime and also a lot of bad habits get formed then too.

Let me emphasize again that the decisions about medication and dosage should be made jointly by the parents, the teacher and the physician.

The last thing I would like to mention about this syndrome is the moral issue. Throughout the country many teachers and parents are in an uproar about "giving kids medicine to make them learn." Let me just mention my feelings about this and you can make your own decision.

It has been well documented for many years that a strep throat can lead to some very serious medical problems if left untreated. Just two of these complications are rheumatic heart disease and a frequently fatal kidney disease, called glomerulonephritis. In all the years that doctors have known about this condition, nobody has ever hesitated giving kids with strep throat a shot of penicillin. As a matter of fact, it would be malpractice not to do so. In other words, *we treat a small disease* (strep throat) *with medication to prevent much more serious complications* (rheumatic heart disease and glomerulonephritis) from resulting. In my opinion, the same situation applies to the hyperkinetic syndrome. In and of itself, this syndrome is rather small and sometimes unimportant, but by treating the kid with medication we can prevent some very serious complications from occurring; failure to learn in school and development of some bad social habits. I can only say if he were my child, there would be no question in my mind, but that I would give the ounce of prevention so the pound of cure would not be needed.

If you suspect your child might have the hyperkinetic syndrome, discuss it with your child's teacher, counselor and physician. I have seen many kids who first present themselves to me at age fourteen or fifteen, having been involved in stealing or fighting. When I talk to their parents and find the kids were hyperkinetic and were never diagnosed or treated, I feel a real tragedy has taken place. These complications were completely preventable. If your child is truly hyperkinetic, make sure he gets the treatment he needs.

CHAPTER XX

The Shy Kid

The shy kid causes a great deal of concern for his parents, and in many cases this concern is quite unnecessary and perhaps even harmful. In our present day society there is a great emphasis on "communication." We hear this word bandied about until we are sick of it! Our society has become preoccupied with communication. There is a great emphasis on talking about how we feel, and about how wrong it is to be a part of the "silent majority." We are repeatedly being told we must make our thoughts and feelings known to other people. New advances are constantly being made to enhance this communication, such as the television-telephone, closed circuit television in education and industry, and new and more complete news coverage, just to name a few.

As you can imagine, a shy kid probably was hardly even noticed in the frontier days of the United States, when people just did their own work from day to day and kept pretty much to themselves. The shy kid just did not stand out then nearly as much as he does now. He sticks out like a sore thumb now, sometimes causing unnecessary alarm and overreaction on the part of parents and teachers.

The overall emphasis in this chapter is to "play down" your approach to the shy kid, and to *gradually encourage* him to be a little more outgoing.

The first and perhaps most common reason for shyness in kids is they are simply copying their parents' shyness. You have no idea how many parents come to me each year complaining that their kid is shy, and yet as I talk with these parents, they can hardly get a word out of their mouths without gulping and looking pale and uncomfortable. It is almost as if they do not realize that they themselves are shy. In other cases, although both parents have outgrown their shyness at present, they readily admit they were exactly like that when they were the kid's age.

If the cause of the kid's shyness is that he is just copying his parents, there is little cause for alarm. The best way of handling this is for parents to make a concerted effort to set a better example for the kid. They should try to be more outgoing and try harder to express their thoughts and ideas more verbally and openly. Having set a better example for their kid, they can gradually, over the years, encourage him to express his ideas more verbally and openly. Keep in mind, however, that change in the kid will come slowly. But that is okay, we are in no hurry. If you are smart you do not run and jump into a swimming pool to find out if it is cold or dangerous—you get in very gradually, and, if it is safe, you proceed further. So it will be with the shy kid. He will test new situations very cautiously, and perhaps with your encouragement, try out new things; if they work out all right he will proceed further. Because he is also most likely sensitive, such methods as "getting on" him, harrassing him, hollering at him, or spanking him, will only make his shyness worse, and he will tend to withdraw even more into himself. With this type of kid, stay away from the forceful approaches—just encourage.

Occasionally I will see a kid who is referred to me because of his shyness, and I will find something very interesting. On interviewing his parents, brothers and sisters I find they are extremely loud and outgoing, perhaps to the point of being obnoxious. The kid himself is completely normal, but by comparison with his parents and his brothers and sisters, he is shy. Very simply, the problem is to help the parents see this kid in proper perspective. It is almost as if this kid "can't get a word in edgewise." Parents therefore can learn to suppress their own communication and invite this kid to join in on the conversation. To put it simply, this kid is not going to be heard until someone else in the family can "shut up."

I would like to make a comment at this point about the "bookworm." Parents sometimes get awfully upset about this kid and then tend to overreact, causing many problems. Like everything else in life, moderation is the key. It is not a question of whether reading a lot is bad for you; it certainly is not, but reading to escape from your problems will not help you to solve them. It is no different than getting drunk to escape a problem. When you are sober again, the problem is still there. Occasionally we see kids who go off into the fantasy world of books because it is just more pleasant than being around the stormy family situation. In this case it is the stormy family problem that needs to be solved, not the kid's reading so much. The question then becomes whether the kid is reading because he likes to read or is he reading to get away from facing problems or responsibilities? When you look at it this way the solution is very simple. If he is reading because he likes to read, fine, let him read as much as he wants. If he is reading as a defense against facing problems, you need to work with your kid at helping him find better solutions to his problems than hiding in a book.

The kid who gets preoccupied with reading, sometimes misses out on the very beneficial and educational things that occur in everyday life.

Another reason for kids being shy and quiet is their parents *want* them to be outgoing. A fact of human nature we have talked about in many other ways is that most of us are naturally stubborn. When somebody pushes us, we automatically have the urge to push back.

I have seen many families like this, but one in particular comes to mind. This was the case of Stan, a fourteen-year-old boy who was referred to me when he was found by his parents participating in what the parents called a "homosexual act." Stan started out right from the beginning, a shy but pleasant kid. Dad had been a football player in college and after college entered the business world and had always been very outgoing and aggressive. Mom was very much that way also. Stan had had a number of ear infections when he was between the ages of one and three, and still was not talking at age three. As you might guess with this kind of parents, they started going overboard right from the beginning. They took Stan to a speech therapist, practiced with him at home, tried to force him to talk, and punished him for being silent. This was the pattern being established in almost every area of Stan's life. Stan was not aggressive about anything, especially eating. Of course, his parents started bugging him about eating—they wanted him to "really dig in." Throughout the years they demanded he get involved in sports (always the most aggressive sports), and be involved in plays and public speaking. And, of course, Stan shoved back. He did not do this in any open way, he just became even more shy and withdrawn. These battles went on for years. The more his parents demanded he be more outgoing and aggressive, the more shy Stan became until finally Stan committed the "ultimate crime": he was found with one of his boyfriends, undressed.

We will talk further in the next chapter about the effeminate boy, but this situation with Stan had nothing to do with sex. It had to do with a power struggle. His parents were trying to force him to be something he did not want to be and Stan's own natural stubbornness was demanding that he was going to do what he wanted to do.

Just let anybody push him and he would show that he could really fight back and get back at his parents "where they live."

How simple this whole problem would have been to prevent! Most certainly, if Stan's parents could have gotten "off their horse" and simply accepted Stan's shyness by developing an attitude of, "I guess that's just how he is," they would have had an excellent chance of Stan's never developing these problems. They could have gradually encouraged Stan to be a little more outgoing and that probably very gradually would have happened.

As I have mentioned, perhaps one of the biggest tragedies in our society is our lack of respect for the individual. We just want everybody to be like us, and that approach has never, in the history of man, been successful. We must have respect for every individual, whether he is our kid, our neighbor, or the man we work with.

Sometimes kids are shy because their self-esteem is low. In Rule 5 we talked about how putting kids down frequently results in kids who feel worthless. Kids who feel worthless show many kinds of behavior such as poor school work, bad behavior at home, in the classroom, and in the community. Certainly kids who feel worthless often act very shy and withdrawn. They frequently feel stupid, and feeling that way, they certainly do not want other people to find out how stupid they are, so they just clam up. Just as the lady who only owns one ragged, old hat is not going to wear it in the Easter Parade, the kid who feels his personality is pretty shabby is going to try to conceal it. He has grown to feel that way because people have been putting him down, criticizing him, making him feel worthless, and making him feel stupid. Notice, I said they have been making him "feel" stupid. For the most part retarded kids are not shy, particularly if they have been raised in a healthy way which has encouraged their self-worth. Regardless of whether a kid is of normal intelligence or below normal intelligence, if somebody has been "putting him down" he is going to act shy and withdrawn. If this is a problem in your family, you need to start looking for your kid's strengths rather than his weaknesses; start looking for the things he does right, instead of all the things he does wrong.

Still another cause for shyness is when parents put up roadblocks to their child's anger. In Rule 4 we talked about the kid who tries to keep his feelings inside because his parents will not let him express them.

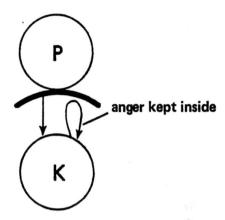

Figure 8. Anger kept inside.

This kid will frequently appear to be shy and withdrawn. The solution is to take the wall down and encourage the kid to *express* his anger (and other feelings) directly and appropriately.

Another kid who will appear to be extremely shy is the kid who is severely mentally disturbed. This kid lives for a large part of the day in his dream world. He is so involved in his fantasies he finds it extremely difficult to come back to reality. Fortunately these cases are rare, and a qualified professional will be your best guide in helping you evaluate this kid. This diagnosis can sometimes be difficult in young kids, particularly when you realize normal kids do a lot of daydreaming and fantasizing.

The last kind of shy kid that I would like to mention is the one whose parents bring him to me saying, "There's nothing wrong with him, he is just lazy." I am mentioning this category because I do not believe in it; I think it is a myth. I have never seen a kid who keeps his feelings inside or who does not learn in school, or who does not talk, because he is lazy. That sometimes is just a convenient excuse parents and teachers sometimes come up with to help explain the kid's behavior. *Laziness in children does not exist.* Certainly kids keep their feelings inside and they do not talk and they do not learn in school, but not because of laziness; rather they are doing it for some other reasons mentioned earlier. Mostly they are shy because somebody is demanding that they not be shy. Remember, I encouraged you earlier to drop that word "why" from your vocabulary when you are talking with kids. The word "lazy" is another word that also needs to be dropped. It has no value in dealing with problems of children.

Throughout this book I have stressed the importance of the individual. Some professionals used the term "individuation" to describe the entire process of kids' growing up. Certainly this "wanting to be myself" is no more evident than in the teenage years. It is said the work of the teenager is to separate himself from his parents; in other words, that is his job at that time in his life. Certainly there are other things he is doing like getting an education, making friends, and learning skills for later on, but probably the most important thing he is doing is learning to become an individual. Kids cannot become individuals if they are just like their parents. If dad is always neat and tidy in his appearance and has shiny shoes, his son feels, to copy that behavior would only have him grow up to be another dad. And he does not want to be another dad, he wants to be himself, a unique individual. He needs to do things differently than dad, he needs to experiment and try new and different things. For the most part teenagers' experimentations are fairly safe and only occasionally do they get into trouble with them. All too often teenagers get into trouble, because their parents will not allow the smaller experimentations, therefore forcing the kid to go into larger experiments. That is like denying your kid a chance to smoke cigarettes, and finding out later that he has gone on to marijuana instead.

What does this all have to do with the shy kid? One of the things the shy kid is trying to do is to say "let me be me; let me be myself, even though I am quiet and not as outgoing as my parents are." When you think of it this way, it is a pretty reasonable request. Like with any other kid, you simply need to capitalize on his strengths rather than his weaknesses. Very frequently shy kids have a great deal of sensitivity which enables them to excel in art, music, or many other fields. Play down their weaknesses and capitalize on their strengths.

CHAPTER XXI

The Effeminate Boy

Nothing is more puzzling, frustrating, or fearful to parents than to see their son growing up with what they consider effeminate traits. Very early in the boy's life they become alarmed and almost panicky over the prospect of how they, two perfectly normal, red-blooded American parents, could produce a "queer" or a "homosexual." They subsequently begin to overreact, to get involved with the kid's behavior and mannerisms, to start demanding he do certain things and not do certain things. The end result is often tragic. Kids who feel worthless tend to act worthless. Parents putting their kid down for his mannerisms, for his interests, and for his attitudes certainly is going to make him feel worthless. Perhaps out of rebellion more than anything, this kid may become a homosexual or a delinquent.

Throughout this chapter most of the things I am saying about the effeminate boy certainly apply to the masculine girl or the "tomboy" as she is called. She is certainly just as susceptible to the pressures and problems I am about to describe to you in dealing with the effeminate boy.

Freud and his successors talked about a certain kind of family which *can* produce a homosexual boy. Typically there is an aggressive, domineering and even "castrating" mother. Father is usually described as passive, weak, and perhaps helpless or dependent. Essentially the two important features of this kind of parental situation is that there are problems with aggression and identification. Let me explain these two in more detail.

In Freud's theory the problem with aggression goes something like this. Mother is so angry and so domineering and is always so "cutting" to the boy that, after years of growing up in this kind of situation, the boy becomes fearful of women. He sees them as threatening and even dangerous. Because his father was always meek, the boy sees men as nonthreatening or safe. For this reason, it is thought, that when this boy grows up he will choose a male as a sexual partner rather than a female; he has learned over the years that men are safe and women are dangerous.

153

The second component of this picture is identification. By that Freud meant, the boy's copying his parents' behavior. In the family described above, this boy will get a somewhat inaccurate view of the role of men and women because he will see his mother as being the domineering one and his father being the passive, weak one. This boy is going to copy his parents pretty much as he grows up. Since he has always seen men as being passive and weak and dependent, he too will become molded in that direction.

What does this all have to do with the effeminate boy? *I certainly do not mean to imply that all effeminate boys are going to be homosexuals.* In fact, it is extremely rare for an effeminate boy to turn out to be homosexual. Most often that is just a phase boys go through and will outgrow if pretty much left alone. It is only when parents start to be critical and try to manipulate the kid's life that they get into trouble. I have mentioned Freud's theory here, not only because it is interesting and relevant to homosexuals, but because it certainly has bearing on how one should approach an effeminate boy. Again, let us look at it in terms of two elements, aggression and identification.

First of all, I do not want to alarm you or cause you any concern if you find you are a couple in which mom tends to be aggressive and dad tends to be somewhat passive. I must emphasize again that that in itself will not cause your boy to grow up to be homosexual. What is important, however, is what mom does with her aggressiveness. If she gets to be a "real pain," and if she is indeed what is commonly called a "nagging bitch," that is going to be a very difficult situation, not only for the boy, but for the husband as well as the rest of the family. If mom is that way, she certainly must make a concerted effort to change her actions for the sake of the entire family. Likewise, if father is extremely passive and lets everybody push him around, including the kids, that is not going to be good for anyone in the family.

I have always been impressed with just how stubborn most people really are. We all tend to want to go our own ways and tend to be very resistant to criticism or suggestions. We all tend to push back when people push us. This is also true with the effeminate boy. Often I have seen a father who was himself a college football star, get so upset with his four-year-old son because the boy was more interested in playing with dolls than in playing football. It is understandable dad would feel bad about that, but it is not his feelings that get him into trouble, it is his actions. What does he do about it? First of all he scolds his son, gives him dirty looks and generally puts him down for liking dolls. Then, to make matters worse, he starts wrestling a lot with his son, making him put on boxing gloves and hitting his son harder than he should, and getting him out by the hour on weekends and evenings to insist that he play baseball and football, two things the little boy just hates. This is where the boy's natural stubbornness comes in. The more dad pushes him toward dad's interests, the more the boy becomes well-entrenched in his effeminate interests.

Sometimes we introduce ideas into kids' heads they have never even thought of. Frequently they will act on these ideas just because we have told them not to. That is like the mother who tells her kid, "Don't ever put pebbles in your ear." The boy has probably never even thought about putting pebbles in his ear, but since his mother has mentioned it and it sounds like an interesting no-no, he gives it a try. We all too often introduce these no-no's by overreacting to a situation. For instance, if you found your four-year-old little boy undressing the little neighbor boy during a play session, and you overreacted to that by getting upset and calling him names, he would get the idea that that must be something pretty great for you to overreact that way. It would be much better to just ignore that situation if you found it or else just to play it down by saying, "Hey, boys, we don't do that sort of thing."

There is a certain amount of healthy experimentation that does and should take place as kids are growing up. Boys are very curious about little girls' bodies, but also about little boys' bodies. Accurate statistics are certainly hard to come by, but most people estimate that as high as 50 percent of all boys have some kind of sexual experimentation with other boys during the growing up years. This most frequently takes place when the boys get their very first interests in sex at age three to four and again after puberty in the early teens. You see many boys have what can be called "homosexual experiences," but are not homosexuals. It is for the most part, the word that bothers us. Despite how open minded we are, and try to be about homosexuality, it is a subject that is basically very uncomfortable for many of us because of the way we were raised. But like prejudices of any kind, it is not our feelings that get us into trouble, it is our actions.

When I was in the Army I saw hundreds of GIs who became very panicky and thought they were "queer" or homosexual because they found themselves having some fond feelings about another man or even some sexy thoughts about him. But neither that nor even having a few homosexual experiences makes a homosexual. A homosexual can be defined as a person who regularly and consistently favors a sexual relationship with a person of the same sex. I said regularly and consistently; that is important. It is important that you parents realize this, so you will not become panicky and act in some ridiculous and even detrimental manner when you discover your son has been experimenting with another boy.

Let me offer in a stepwise fashion some suggestions for dealing with the effeminate boy. First of all, it is important to decide if there really is a problem or if it is just that dad or mom is pretty hung up on having a supermasculine little boy. If you look at the situation carefully you probably will discover there is not a thing wrong with your little boy and nothing needs to be done. If you do feel your son, however, does tend to be somewhat effeminate, be extremely careful not to overreact. You must keep your prejudices and fears under control and try not to let them influence your actions. Keep in mind that in order for a boy to grow up to be "manly" he must have men around during his growing up years. Dad's being around a little bit more probably would be helpful. But if that is impossible because of divorce, long separations or death, a father substitute can be made available. "Big Brother" organizations have been set up for this purpose and do provide some masculine identifications for young boys. Your boy needs a man to pattern himself after and there are many ways to provide that. Certainly it would be all right for you to *gently* encourage masculine interests such as sports, boy scouts and hard physical work.

It is important *not to criticize* or discourage the things your kid is doing that you consider effeminate. Just like criticizing your child for stuttering will make the stuttering worse, your criticizing your boy for his effeminate hand gestures will draw more attention to them and probably make them worse. Likewise, forbidding your boy to play with dolls is only going to make him want to play with dolls all the more.

Lastly, if you find you just cannot decide whether there is a problem or you do not know what you should do about it, seek professional help, but do it without your kid's knowing about it. This is not the kind of situation where you want to take your son in to the family doctor and in front of the boy ask the doctor if he thinks your son is a "little girly." Most often you will find it is your hang-up and if you leave the kid alone he will grow up just fine.

There was an excellent expression that was popular a few years ago that I think has a lot of meaning. The expression was, "Different strokes for different folks." We do not all have to think, talk, feel, and act alike to be happy. I am sure what you want most in life is for your kid to grow up happy and successful, not for him to grow up and be exactly like you. Not all boys are going to grow up to be football players or truck drivers who use foul language and sport a tattoo on each arm. That is not important. What is important, however, is that your son be allowed to find his own interests in life and his own style of living, providing it does not infringe on anybody else's style of living. If you have respect for your son as an individual and respect his individual differences, then it is likely that problems will not develop.

CHAPTER XXII

The Fearful Kid

Like so many other problems we face with children, if we handle their fears properly they will disappear, but if we handle them improperly the fears will get worse and perhaps even cause other problems. I would like to discuss this question of fears of children by describing four categories of fear, why they are present and the best way to handle them. These four main categories of fear are the "normal" fears, the fear of separation, the fear of bodily harm, and the fear of exposure.

Let us take first the so-called "normal" fears of childhood. These are called "normal" fears because they are things many of us have been afraid of at some time in our lives, but probably with some help from our parents, we have gotten over them. It is very common for children to be afraid of dogs, snakes, and many other animals. In a way we can consider these the fear of the unknown and new and different things are frequently a cause of fear for a child. Hundreds of years ago, when the American Indians first saw an eclipse of the sun, it was reported that they ran screaming wildly out of their villages, fearing the world was coming to an end. They were afraid because something was happening they did not understand, something that was entirely new to them. But apparently as the Indians were able to pass on this information from one generation to the next, it no longer was frightening. Such is the case with kids who are exposed to new experiences and new things. The first time a kid sees a person dressed up for Halloween he is apt to become frightened, just as he might become frightened the first time he comes close to a big dog. Overprotective parents sometimes have very scared children because they never allow their kids to be frightened, and then to get over it.

Because as adults we can certainly understand these "normal" kinds of fear, we are more apt to deal with them correctly. We will comfort and reassure the kid and show him the Halloween face is just a mask or the dog is friendly and hold his hand while we encourage him to "pet the nice doggie."

With other fears however, because we do not always understand them ourselves, we are more apt to deal with them incorrectly. Let me describe a case to you that demonstrates some important points. Several years ago a couple came to see me with their twelve-year-old daughter. It seemed their daughter had been seeing another psychiatrist for the last year and a half for her "night phobia," without any success. I asked the girl to wait in the waiting room and had her parents tell me in detail of the girl's problems and what they had been doing about it.

It seems that eight years ago, when Debbie was only four years old, she began waking up at night very fearful. There was nothing upsetting happening in the family at that time and the parents could not understand why the child was so afraid. Within a few days the waking up progressed to waking up and crying and acting very scared. For lack of something better to do mother began getting up each night with the little girl and going into her room to comfort her and help her get back to sleep. She would stroke Debbie's head and back and say soothing, comforting things to her and after a while Debbie would go back to sleep. However, despite all mom's efforts, Debbie's nightly waking and crying continued and, as a matter of fact, it got a little more difficult each night to get Debbie to go back to sleep and the ordeal began lasting a little longer. This went on for many months and mom was getting tired of getting up in the middle of the night with Debbie, so when Debbie would wake up, mother would bring her into mom and dad's bed. This went on for several weeks and every time Debbie came to mom and dad's bed she seemed to be much more comfortable and to be able to sleep, but every time mom would try insisting on Debbie's sleeping in her own bed, she would start crying and become fearful again. As you are reading this description I am giving you, you are probably seeing the handwriting on the wall. Debbie was leading her parents right down the garden path, but they could not see that because they were right in the middle of it. If they only could have backed off and been a little bit more objective about what was happening, they could have prevented the further deterioration.

Years had gone by and Debbie was still waking up at night and crying and carrying on, disrupting not only her parents' night sleep, but the other children's as well. Finally, dad was getting so run down from not sleeping well he could hardly do a day's work at the office.

He started to spend evenings and whole nights away from home just to get away from the turmoil there, and when he was home he slept on the sofa in the living room. Repeated attempts to get Debbie back to her own bed at night and to prevent her from coming into the parents' bed always ended in disaster. That is, Debbie would scream and cry and carry on so long that mom and dad would finally give in and let her have her way.

This went on for six and one half years before the family sought professional help. They took Debbie to a child psychiatrist who was trained in the Freudian manner. He told the parents there were some deep, dark secrets down in Debbie's unconscious that needed to come out and he would help Debbie by seeing her twice a week and talking with her and doing "play therapy." The parents repeatedly asked if there was something they could do to help, but were regularly told there was nothing they could do until he, the psychiatrist, was able to somehow magically deal with her deep, dark secrets. He started to work, but after a year and a half of seeing Debbie twice per week and getting nowhere, he apparently gave up. As a matter of fact, it was Debbie's parents who gave up because they felt they were running out of time and money. Debbie was now almost twelve years old and the family's problem was still continuing. They tried for several months on their own after seeing the first psychiatrist, but nothing changed so they decided to try again and came to see me.

Many interesting things have happened since the days of Freud with respect to dealing with fears. It used to be a person would go to a psychoanalyst with a fear of high places, and the analyst and the patient would talk about the patient's fears of high places for weeks, months, and frequently years. They would dig around in the patient's "unconscious," talk about his dreams and his fantasies and his sex life, and then finally the analyst would encourage the patient to gradually start out with some small heights and work his way up to some truly high places. Because there was a relationship there by then, the patient would give it a try and things would work out pretty well. He would suddenly find his fear of high places had disappeared. He also discovered at that time that five-ten years had gone by and about fifty thousand dollars which he used to call his own, now belonged to the analyst. Since those days, many psychiatrists have come to question whether those five years and fifty thousand dollars were really necessary and have wondered if they just could not get to know the patient briefly and start encouraging him, very gradually, to start climbing some higher and higher places. Indeed, this approach has proven very effective in the hands of some professionals.

Let us get back to Debbie and her parents. Right at the beginning I told Debbie's parents I was sorry to hear about Debbie's deep, dark secrets, but I did not think there was much I could do about them. It was her behavior, not her secrets, that was causing the problem.

It sure seemed to me that for the last eight years Debbie's parents had been doing an awful lot of things to reinforce Debbie's behavior. Remember in Rule 3 I talked about my continuing to bang my head on the wall as long as the gold coins kept falling. It seemed to me Debbie's carrying on every night was getting her a lot of gold coins in the form of attention, sympathy, and even getting dad kicked out of his bed (Debbie was sore at dad because he would not feel as sorry for her as mom would). I tried to explain to these parents how they were accidentally encouraging Debbie's problem to continue, but they found it pretty hard to understand. Most of all they found it difficult to accept because another psychiatrist had been telling them for a year and a half a completely different story, namely the one about the deep, dark secrets and how the parents could do nothing to help out.

After the first visit I told them they need not bring Debbie back to see me, but that I wanted to see them once a week until Debbie's problem disappeared. Well, it took two months for these parents to trust me enough to give my program a try. The program I am talking about was nothing spectacular, it was simply based on my belief that if Debbie's behavior was not getting her so much, Debbie would give it up. I explained to these parents that it would be necessary for them to confront Debbie, not so much in words, but in actions. In short, what they would have to do was to make up their minds they were going to have a couple of sleepless nights while Debbie would throw her temper tantrums, but if they were able to stand it, the problem would be solved. Very simply their instructions were to go home and that night tell Debbie that from now on she was going to sleep in her bed and they were going to sleep in their bed and it was the grownups that were going to run the show from now on. Mom and dad were to go to bed at the usual time and were to close the door and lock it. If Debbie woke up during the night and cried, screamed, carried on or turned green, mom and dad were not to make any noise or to leave their bed. We further agreed no matter how long Debbie's behavior continued, mom and dad would consistently go to their bed at night and stay there quietly until morning.

From then on things went as predicted. The first night Debbie cried and screamed, came out in the hallway and banged on her parents' door, and kept it up for about four hours until she fell asleep on the hallway floor. The next morning Debbie's parents walked out of their room and stepped over her and continued their day as if nothing had happened. The next night Debbie awoke and cried for about half an hour and went back to sleep in her own bed. From then on Debbie never had a problem sleeping and the entire family once again enjoyed peaceful, quiet nights.

There are many lessons to be learned from this case. First of all, Debbie's mother was trying to comfort Debbie for the purpose of discouraging her crying at night, but in fact she was encouraging Debbie's fears by giving her all that attention. You must be very careful in dealing with kids' fears not to be too understanding. For example, when your kids are very little and first hear thunder and see lightning and start crying. It is going to be much more supportive for them to have you say, "Oh, that's no big deal," and continue what you are doing rather than for you to go over to the kids and hold them and protect them and stroke them and soothe them. What frequently happens is that kids misinterpret what you are doing and get the idea you, too, are scared.

Another lesson I have learned about fears is that once the fear has developed, there may need to be a confrontation to finally get the kid over it. The confrontation came in Debbie's case when her parents finally just had to tell her they were sorry she was scared at night, but after all they needed their night's sleep and she would have to handle that on her own. Of course, the kid is not going to accept that without a fight, but once he knows you are really going to stick to what you said, he will "hang it up."

We have talked about the category of "normal" fears of childhood. They most frequently peak about the age of three of four, but can continue longer, particularly if they are not handled correctly.

The second category of fear is the fear of separation. Separation fear is frequently of two types, either the parents' leaving the kid or the kid's leaving the parents. It is absolutely essential that if your kid is to grow up, you are going to have to start leaving him at some time or another. You have the right to have some free time of your own and you will need to get out as he is growing up. Also, you are going to have many responsibilities to perform that will require your being away from your child. The kid might be fearful when you first leave him, say, with a babysitter, but if you will make up your mind you are not going to be manipulated or intimidated by his crying and carrying on and having temper tantrums, you will just leave the house and that will be that. There are some basic guidelines to follow in dealing with any kind of separation. It is important for parents, not kids, to call the shots. Also it is important to start small and work up. Your first time out of the house should not be for two weeks, it should be more like five minutes to go to the neighbor's house to borrow a cup of sugar. It is always a good idea to tell your kid exactly where you are going to be and for how long. If you start out and work up gradually you will not have any difficulty. There are certain times in kids' lives when it is more difficult for them to be away from their parents. Probably between the ages of two and five your kid might have his most difficult time. At that age he is old enough to know you are gone, but not old enough to know you are coming back and he might become unusually frightened. That is why in many hospitals they avoid elective surgery between the ages of two and five, and if they do need to perform surgery on a child that age, they will have some facility for the parents to stay with their kid (rooming in).

Like many other things, timing is essential. How long you will be gone from your kid should be based on his age, his maturity, and his ability to understand. Frequently kids under the age of five have a hard time tolerating their parents' being gone over two weeks, whereas a ten year old might easily be able to handle his parents' being away for a month or two. Of course a great deal depends on with whom you are leaving the kid and how competent and capable the babysitter is. It is important your babysitter fully understand your approach to your kid and how she is expected to handle him.

One of the biggest problems kids face on leaving their parents comes on the first day of school. The greater the reluctance of mom and dad to let the kid go from the nest, the more likely will be the chance of the kid's developing a problem over going to school. If the kid finds out his crying and carrying on will keep him home from school, he is liable to do it very frequently. Just as if he sees his coughing or com-

plaining of a stomachache keeps him home with mom, he probably
will have a lot of stomachaches. On the other hand, if mom can use the
approach "I'm sorry to hear about your stomachache Chuck, but
that's life, you're going to school anyway," she will prevent some major problems from developing. Certainly it is understandable how a kid
who has been home with mom for the first five years of his life would
not want to go to school. What is not understandable is mom's letting
him stay home. The so-called fears and phobias can very quickly turn
into manipulations and we need to prevent that.

The third category of fear is the fear of bodily harm. In the chapter
on discipline I talked about how kids see many things in grandiose
terms and how they sometimes fear spanking as if they were going to
be murdered. Kids become very frightened of all kinds of violence, but
particularly when the violence is right in their own home. Seeing a
blood-curdling movie at the theater or watching a horror show on
television is going to be temporarily upsetting, but he probably will
get over that in a few hours. It is the fear he experiences from the
"real violence" at home that is more permanently destructive. Some
good examples of this are mom's violent temper when she hollers and
throws things or dad's own brand of violence coming in the form of
spankings or even beatings. Obviously, I do not need to tell you what
the solution to that kind of fear is . . .

Another kind of fear of bodily harm is that children are very much
afraid of their own anger. They know their self-control is weak and
are fearful they might lose control and really hurt somebody. By setting limits for our kids we reassure them that even if they cannot control themselves, somebody will be around big enough and strong
enough to control them. Very frequently boys going through puberty,
in experiencing their new strength, become afraid they will not be able
to keep it under control. That is why athletics is so important at that
age as a way to "drain off" some of that physical energy.

The last category of fear kids experience is the fear of exposure or
the fear of someone's finding out what they are really thinking. Little
boys, particularly around the ages of three to five, are starting to have
some sexy ideas about mom. It is then that they become fearful of
dad's finding out just what they are thinking. In a study on teenagers
undergoing anesthesia, their biggest concern was that when they were
put to sleep they might reveal something of their thoughts (particularly sexual ones).

Remember you need to be firm. Sometimes the best and most re-assuring thing for a kid who is scared, is to see that his mom or dad is not going to make any big deal about it. For the most part when kids start getting too many benefits (gold coins) from their being fearful, the fears only continue and multiply.

CHAPTER XXIII

The Tense Kid

In this chapter I would like to talk to you about the tense or the nervous kid. We hardly ever have a problem spotting this kid; he is frequently noticed by his actions. Often he will have little habits that call his nervousness to our attention, like biting his nails or exhibiting facial twitches, or waking up at night having nightmares. It is a lot easier to spot these kids than it is to understand and know how to help them. If you can recognize the source of the tension, it then becomes quite obvious what you need to do about it.

The first and by far the most common situation that causes a kid to be tense is the kid whose parents overreact in many ways, but in particular, punish too severely. This kid goes through life walking on eggshells or acting like at any moment he is liable to step on a landmine. That is not an imaginary thing he is experiencing either. Many times in his life, he has learned almost anything can set mom or dad off, and once they are set off, he will suffer. This is the kid who is tense because he lives constantly in a tense, explosive situation. Further, the more severe and the more unpredictable the punishments are, the more tense the kid will be.

This brings us to another source of tension for kids and that is the predictability or the consistency of the world in which they live. There was an interesting experiment done a few years ago that nicely makes the point. The experimenter took several monkeys and placed them in specially designed cages. Every hour on the hour (for eight hours each day), the monkeys would get an electric shock through the metal floor they were standing on. The monkeys were taught to stop the shock by pressing a button in their cages. After several weeks of this experiment the monkeys were studied very carefully and it was found that no physical or psychological problems developed. Then the experiment was changed slightly. The same monkeys were kept in the same cages with the same amount of current, but instead of the electric shock coming hourly, it came in a completely unpredictable manner. Whereas before, the monkeys could stop the shock and then relax for another hour, in the new experiment they could not relax because they constantly had to be on guard for another shock. There was no predictability. After two weeks of the second experiment, all the monkeys were found to have developed stomach ulcers. I think this experiment shows you just how important consistency or predictability is in our lives. It is important for all of us, but it is even more important for kids. If your son's bedtime is at 7:30 tonight, it should be at 7:30 every night.

Another source of tension in kids is when their parents do not control them. A prime example of this is the "spoiled kid" who frequently gets his way and rarely has limits set for him. Try for a moment to put yourself in the skin of a seven-year-old boy who is told to go to bed. Let us suppose further that this little boy starts complaining and whining and his parents say, "All right, a little longer," but they repeatedly let the boy set his own bedtime. The boy probably feels that if his parents cannot even get him to bed on time, how are they going to control him in other ways, particularly when he is angry. He knows he cannot control his anger, and if he sees his parents are not able to control him, then he really gets uncomfortable. Kids feel much more secure and comfortable when they know there are firm limits.

Another important cause of tension in kids is when there is some kind of overstimulation going on in the family. Usually this overstimulation is in the form of some kind of provocative or sexual behavior. The two most common examples of overstimulation are bed-sharing and a lack of modesty among family members. There is no intention on mom's part of being provocative or sexually stimulating when she is taking a bath and has left the door open. It is just something she has not thought about and therefore is not very careful about. The end result, nevertheless, is a kid who is sexually overstimulated, resulting in his being tense and nervous.

Our constantly bugging and harassing them, can be another cause of tension in kids. Again, this usually is not intentional but it happens nevertheless and can be just as destructive. It frequently results in a vicious cycle. For example, your daughter bites her nails because she is tense—you repeatedly bug her about it because you do not like the way it looks. The bugging in turn makes your daughter more tense resulting in her biting her nails even more—and around and around you go. You need to do something about this awful situation. But do not attack the nailbiting; attack the source of the problem, your bugging the kid.

Another reason for a kid's being tense is when he is faced with the fear of separation. Think of how a kid must feel when his parents are not getting along and are having lots of fights. Not only is he going to be tense because of the tension in the family, but he will also be tense because he is afraid his parents will split up and he will be "left out in the cold." Sometimes parents use this fear of separation as a cruel threat in hopes it will modify their kid's behavior. I once saw a mother who, each time her daughter misbehaved, would put her in the car and drive her to the gates of the orphan home and threaten to leave her there if she did not straighten up. That kind of approach only makes kids more tense and their behavior less acceptable.

Certainly there will be separations kids will need to face. But if you prepare your child for the separation and be completely honest with him, he will have a much easier time of it.

The last cause of the tense kid is simply that tension is contagious. After half an hour of talking with a person who stutters, I usually start to stutter a little. Or perhaps you have noticed yourself get fidgety after talking with somebody who is quite nervous. Sometimes kids pick up their nervousness just by being around a parent who is quite tense. Of course, the obvious way to prevent that from happening is by having the parent get some help with his own problem.

There are many reasons why kids become tense or nervous. Once you become aware of the problem, do not just sit back and hope it will go away. Actively seek the reason behind your kid's being tense and, in particular, look very carefully at what you are doing. If you correct what you are doing wrong, your kid's tension will usually disappear very quickly.

CHAPTER XXIV

Losing Someone

An absolutely essential part of living is that sooner or later we must lose someone. Whether it be your child's losing a pet or a playmate, losing a parent through divorce or death, or even a temporary loss such as parents' going on vacation, it is an extremely important and meaningful event in your child's life. Whether the loss is temporary or permanent, your child will need your assistance to help him through the difficult time. The closer and the more meaningful that person was in your child's life, the more difficult it will be for him to get through it successfully. Certainly another factor in your child's getting through a loss successfully is his age. Losing a parent or a close relative is difficult at any age, but losing him when you are just a kid is even tougher. In fact, it is safe to say the younger the kid, the more difficulty he might have with the loss. All too often a parent's not knowing how to help his kid through a significant loss can end in tragedy. It is not at all unusual for a loss in the kid's early life to cause permanent damage. I am not trying to alarm you, but I am trying to stress the importance of your helping your kid through these difficult times. As I indicated in earlier chapters, facing a crisis and getting through it successfully can add greatly to emotional maturity.

Let me now suggest some things you can do in order to help your kid through this difficult time:

1. *Prepare him in advance if you can.* Most of the losses in your kid's life are predictable. If you know you are going to be moving away from the area in which you are living, you know in advance your child will be losing his friends. Do not wait till the moving day arrives to talk to him about it. Let him know as soon as you know, and in that way you can prepare him for it emotionally. The same thing is true with death. It is unusual for a young, healthy parent to die suddenly. Certainly that happens, but it is rare. More often, however, a parent, grandparent, or some other person close to your child will be ill for a time before his death. That is the time to start talking to your kid about it and preparing him in advance for that painful situation. As a matter of fact, I think it is important to talk to kids about death, even when you do not suspect it will take place in the near

169

future. Children are extremely naive about life and death. It is almost as if they think their parents and grandparents are going to live forever. It is probably because we, their parents, find it so painful to talk about death, that we do not bring up the subject. But death follows life just as certainly as night follows day and at some time in your child's life he will need to face the death of a loved one. Therefore it is a good idea to talk about it even though you do not think it is likely in the immediate future.

2. *Be completely honest.* I have seen some very tragic situations where kids were told mom or dad did not really die, they just went away for a while. Sometimes our religious notions about life after death are not only confusing to us, but are quite misleading to our children. Regardless of how you feel about life after death, or the "hereafter," it is important to let your kid know that death, at least here on earth, is quite permanent. Remember, your kid will not be able to do a successful job of mourning unless he realizes death is permanent.

3. *Keep the feelings alive after the loss.* Talking about the loss before, during, and afterwards, enables your child to work it out in a much healthier way. It is particularly important to talk to him about his feelings for the person he has lost. Perhaps an analogy might be an abcess. If nothing is done to it, it all too often will stay beneath the surface and fester. However, if it is opened and drained it can heal over very nicely with very little scar remaining. If the child loses someone close to him and the feelings do not get talked about, the feelings will lie there and cause problems. If the feelings get talked about over a period of time after the loss, there is a good chance your child will not only get over it completely, but will be even better prepared for other losses in his future life.

Let me tell you about an important study done by a psychiatrist, Doctor Derek Miller, in London a few years ago. Doctor Miller worked very closely with the school system and had noticed for several years that children who experienced a significant loss in their family, usually the death of a parent, adjusted very poorly afterwards. Not only did their schoolwork suffer, but they frequently deteriorated socially and occasionally became delinquent. Working on the premise that kids should be able to get over it if someone helps them with their feelings, Doctor Miller set up a large study in the schools. In one group of children who had lost a parent (Group A), he did nothing but observed them over a period of several years. With the second group (Group B), Doctor Miller had the kids' teachers say something to them (on a daily basis) which would remind them of the loss of their parents and also encourage them to talk about their feelings. The teacher might say, "Gee, Johnny, it must be pretty tough at home now without dad there." The teacher was helping to keep the kid's feelings alive about dad, even though dad was gone. The results were not only very interesting, but give us some concrete evidence of how important it is to help our kids with their losing someone.

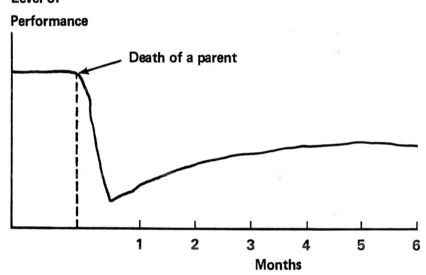

Group A: Nothing done to help with the loss.

Figure 9. Result of losing a parent.

Group A represents the first group of kids, where nothing was done to help them through their loss. As you can see, their performance and behavior dropped dramatically right at the time of the death of one of their parents, and over a six month period it gradually improved, but never (on the average) regained its original level. Some of the girls became promiscuous and a number of the girls and boys became delinquent. Their schoolwork, too, was a reflection of the emotional difficulty they continued to have.

Group B represents the kids with whom the teacher worked on a daily basis. As you can see, they too went into a significant slump at the time of the death of a parent, but over a six month period they not only pulled out of it, but returned completely to their previous level of performance. Do not get the idea the teacher did psychotherapy with these kids, nor did she spend a great deal of time helping them. The teacher only said one or two sentences to the kid each day. What was important was that it was just enough to keep the kid's feelings alive and to get some of the kid's feelings out in the open.

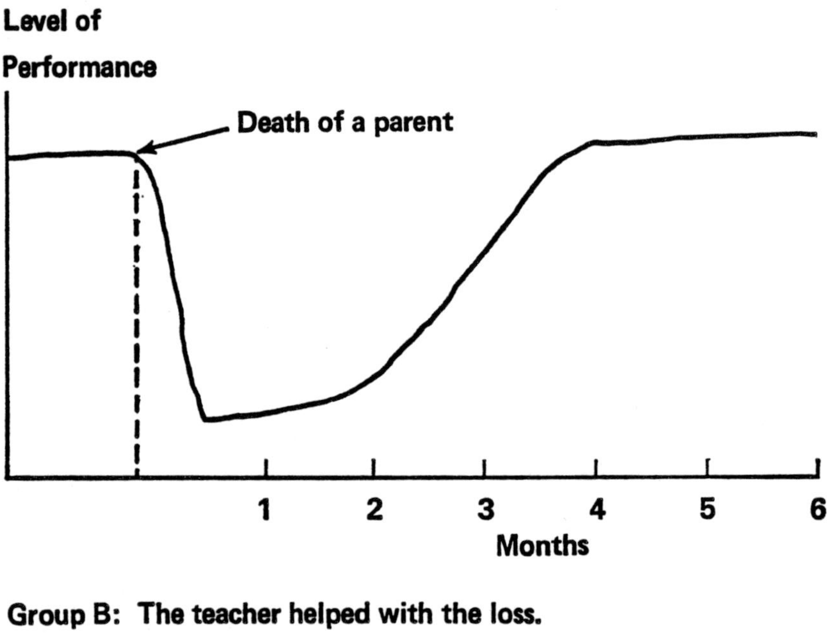

Level of

Performance

Death of a parent

1   2   3   4   5   6

Months

Group B: The teacher helped with the loss.

Figure 10. Teacher's intervention with parental loss.

That old saying, "Big boys don't cry," can be very destructive at a time like this. Big boys do cry and little boys cry, and parents need to encourage, not discourage, their kids to have a good cry over losing someone. This is one time when it is *healthy* for everyone in the family to sit down and have a good cry, if the loss truly effects everyone in the family.

4. *Do not run from the loss—face it.* We all have a tendency to run from things that are painful to face directly. All too often I have seen men, following the deaths of their wives, begin drinking a great deal or running around frantically with other women, or becoming "work-aholics." This is done in a desperate attempt not to face the pain of

losing their wives. If your son's puppy gets run over by a car, do not run out and buy him a new one, or at least do not do it for several months. Let him experience the pain of death and help him with his feelings. You are not being cruel, you are doing what will be best for him in the long-run.

Perhaps you have had the experience of having a good friend of yours lose someone important to him. You probably have felt very uncomfortable in going to your friend and expressing your sympathy and spending some time with him. In fact, many people avoid someone who is in mourning. That is the time when he really needs people more, not less. The mourner often feels like his friends have deserted him, and rightly so. They have.

5. *Do not let your child blame himself.* I saw a seven-year-old boy named Eddy recently because he was still acting quite depressed and withdrawn almost a year after his father died. It is hard to know how long after a significant loss it will take for a kid to "pull out of it," but usually after six months to a year you should see progress in that direction. Little Eddy was making no progress. He was just as depressed and withdrawn one year after dad's death as he had been shortly after it happened. Eddy's mother tried talking with him about dad's death on many occasions, but she said his feelings seemed to be "stuck inside." I started seeing Eddy regularly and as we talked, it seemed to me he was blaming himself for his father's death. Eddy's dad had died suddenly of a heart attack and certainly Eddy had no part to play in it, but in Eddy's mind he was somehow responsible. One day, while we were talking about it, Eddy broke down and cried profusely. He went on to tell me how, for a long time, when he was very angry at dad, he would say to himself, "I wish he was dead." And then when it finally happened, Eddy felt it was his wishing death on his father that had caused it. This is what we call "magical thinking." We all do it to a certain extent, but kids do it a lot. They think wishing something can make it happen. Once I was able to talk to Eddy and explain to him about his father's heart attack and about blood vessels clogging up and so on, he was able to see he had no part in his dad's death. He was able to stop blaming himself for it, and subsequently pulled out of his depression.

This kind of magical thinking is frequently a problem when a kid loses one of his parents through divorce. Even though his parents may have been fighting before the kid was even born, he somehow blames himself for their splitting up. This is another reason for being completely honest with a kid. If mom and dad split up because of dad's drinking, it is important for the child to know about dad's drinking problem. If he is not able to understand the true reasons for the divorce, he is more likely to blame himself and that will make it more difficult for him to go through the loss successfully.

You can see just how vital a parent's role is in helping his kid work through losing someone. If you make a little extra effort in helping your child through these difficult times, you have an excellent chance of preventing any further difficulty.

The adopted child has also experienced a loss in his life, and even though he may have been too young to remember it as such, sooner or later he will know something happened to his original parents, and that may cause him some difficulty. I think therefore it is essential to keep in mind the steps I have mentioned above. All too often parents put off the painful business of talking with their adopted kid until he is eighteen and about to leave the family. Then the kid feels (and understandably so) that his adoptive parents have betrayed him by not telling him the truth sooner. In essence he feels he has been lied to by omission. Therefore it is a good idea to start talking to your adopted kid about it when he is old enough to understand. For many kids this will be as early as four or five years of age. Tell him the truth about what you know of his real parents. And also tell him why you wanted to adopt a child. Help him to understand that "Mom and Dad" are the people who raise you and love you, and not just the people that bring you into the world. It is likely that an adopted child is going to have more difficulty than the average child with subsequent losses he may experience. He therefore will need your help even more in helping him with his feeling. But if you will follow the above guidelines, you have every reason to expect that he will be able to get through it successfully.

You can prevent further difficulties following a loss if you will prepare your child and discuss the loss openly and honestly. Encourage him to talk about his feelings and help him face the loss without blaming himself. With your help he will get through the difficult time successfully.

CHAPTER XXV

Nuisance Problems

By nuisance problems I mean the little, everyday, irritating confrontations we have with our kids over things like their keeping their rooms clean, going to bed, getting up in the morning and handling their allowance. There is one overriding principle you must keep in mind when you are dealing with all the million and one nuisance problems you have with your kids. You must find solutions to these problems in such a way as to make sure the job gets done, but without creating a lot of hard feelings over it. I could club my daughter over the head to make her pick up her clothes, and she would probably do it. But is that really the only thing I want, for her to pick up her clothes? Of course not. I would like for her to pick up her clothes, but I would also like to maintain peace and harmony in the family. I will have to find some kind of solution that will get her to pick up her clothes, but do it in such a way that peace and harmony in the family can continue.

Millions of families go from day to day making each other miserable over little, insignificant things. Remember in Rule I when I talked about the Army sergeant who bugged his sons about their hair until they finally rebelled and got arrested for drug abuse? Many of the everyday little nuisance problems we fight over with our kids are just not worth it, and certainly they are not worth having the whole family go down the drain. Let me emphasize again that you must find solutions to these nuisance problems in such a way that there will be a minimum of hard feelings.

Keep in mind, however, that if your kid has a particular problem such as throwing his clothes around, there is an excellent chance somebody else at home is setting a bad example. For the most part, if you set good examples yourself for cleanliness and neatness in the home, and you do not harass your kids about it, they will follow your lead and tend to be neat and tidy themselves.

A third and last point before I get into the specific kinds of nuisance problems is, that *you need to be very specific* with your kids about what their responsibilities are, when you want them done, and what the consequences will be if they are not done. Saying to your kid,

"Earl, you better start keeping your room clean," is a pretty meaningless statement. It is like telling your kid to come home when it is dark. There is just too much room for misinterpretation and that kind of statement just guarantees that sooner or later the parents and Earl are going to have a fight over Earl's room not being clean.

While we are on the subject of keeping the room clean we might as well go into it in more detail. My daughters and I had a lot of hard feelings over their rooms being clean for several years, and then my wife and I found a solution that works pretty well. We sat the kids down and told them in detail what was expected. We told them that each morning they were expected to get up, and before they went off to school, to make their beds and pick up their things from the floor. In other words, on the weekdays we expected only a casual straightening, but explained to them exactly what we meant by that. We then set aside Saturday morning as the routine time for their rooms to get a good cleaning. Again, we described in detail what we meant. Further we told the kids they were to get up first thing each Saturday morning and start cleaning. Of course, they were allowed out of their rooms to go to the bathroom and have breakfast, but they would not be allowed out for anything else until the room was inspected by mom or dad. The consequences were clearly laid out that they would stay in their rooms until they were clean, even if that took the entire weekend. Of course, my younger, stubborn daughter had to check out my sincerity the first time. She played around in her room all day Saturday and finally the confrontation came at seven in the evening when she asked to come out and watch television. When again she learned she could not manipulate us, she very quickly started to work and cleaned up her room. From then on my kids' rooms have usually been clean, and most important of all, we have avoided the hard feelings that used to go along with that chore.

It is never necessary to use threats. When I use the word threat I mean something that will be scary to the kid. There is a difference between his facing the consequences of his actions and his being threatened. When you drive your car for example, you know if you go through a stop sign, there is a reasonable likelihood that you might have an accident or get a ticket. You of course still have that option of crashing the stop sign or stopping for it, but once you know the consequences you will most likely get in a habit of stopping at stop signs. You know no traffic cop is going to jump out and beat up on you, or shoot you, or do you some bodily harm even if you do go through the stop sign. It is not fear that keeps you from crashing stop signs, it is understanding the logical consequences of your actions. It is amazing how many parents think fear is the only way to keep their kids in line. That is a totally unnecessary and in fact harmful way to control your kids. If you give them a choice, and they understand the consequences of their actions, they will almost always make the right decisions. I did not threaten to beat my daughters if they did not clean their rooms, I just told them they had the choice of either cleaning their rooms or spending the weekend in them until the rooms were cleaned.

I said earlier rewards are just the opposite side of the same coin as punishments, and they therefore have no place in nuisance problems. Mom does not get a dollar every time she cooks a meal, so why should your son get paid for straightening his room? Families are a team and everybody in the family needs to pull together, and we pull together by each of us taking care of our own responsibilities.

There is a tendency for many parents who have grown up with a lot of hard work, many chores and responsibilities, to want their kids to have lots of work when they are growing up. Please keep in mind there is a middle ground that is probably ideal for your kids. They should not be loaded down with work, chores, and housework, and yet on the other hand they should not be totally free of responsibility. You need to remind yourself that the primary job of a kid growing up is to get an education, to learn to get along with other people, and to have fun. Certainly he needs chores and responsibilities, but let us not forget he needs some time to play also. You should strive for a healthy balance between hard work and play.

Getting the family up in the morning and getting the kids off to school is frequently the first upsetting confrontation of the day, and certainly a needless one. Suppose one of your kids is awfully pokey in the morning. You could handle that by just bugging him from the time he gets up to the time he goes out the door, but that is probably just going to make both of you miserable. Who wants to start out the day like that; it is likely to ruin the rest of the day for both of you. And yet so many parents do that with their kids every morning of their lives. Wouldn't it be so much better to tell your kid exactly what you expect him to do and by when, and then also tell him if he does not make it to school on time, what you are going to do about it? In other words, give him a choice—either he gets to school on time or he faces the consequences. A possible consequence for not getting to school on time might be your kid's having to stay in his room after school that day. I can assure you, if given a choice, your kid will not want to spend too many days in his room after school. He probably very quickly will elect to get up in the morning and "get cracking."

A nice technique I have found which avoids some of the confrontations is to get your kid his own alarm clock, teach him how to set it, and make him responsible for getting himself up in the morning. Mom, do not take that as a suggestion from me that you should sleep in. Your presence and your smiling face is much needed by your entire family. Of course, you are going to be up to put breakfast on the table, and it is also a nice time for the family members to visit with each other a little bit before starting their day. Again, I am suggesting you completely avoid the harassment.

Your kid's allowance may be one of the things which gets to be a real nuisance. It probably should be started at about the age of three or four and gradually increased in amount as he gets older. With increasing allowance, of course, he is given increasing responsibility for it. As I mentioned previously, at first his allowance ought to be used entirely as he wishes, perhaps then, after he starts school his school supplies should come out of the allowance. Once again you are not going to tell him he must spend ten cents on paper and seventy-five cents on the show, etc. It would be much better to say to your eight year old, that he will be getting a dollar a week and from now on he is expected to take care of his entertainment and his school supplies. Let him figure out the details and be responsible for handling them. As he gets older his clothing should come out of his allowance as well as the responsibility for shopping for it. If your fourteen-year-old son wants to wear ragged jeans and chooses to spend his allowance on records instead of clothing, I would let him do that. Remember, once you give him the money, he can use it in any legal way he sees fit.

I would encourage you to be very cautious about stopping your kid's allowance or taking it away for misconduct. It is reasonable if your son breaks his sister's dollhouse, for him to be expected to pay for it. Do not stop his allowance for bad behavior and certainly do not stop it for bad grades. He needs his allowance in order to learn to handle money.

Just a word about doing dishes. That is a reasonable chore for kids and kids do need chores to add to their sense of responsibility and their sense of accomplishment. But dishes are something kids and parents fight over a lot and there is no reason for it. Probably it will not work out very well, for example, if you send your two daughters in to do the dishes each night. You know in advance what will happen. They will start bickering and fighting and complaining that the other one is not doing her job. It would be much better for you to work out a plan so only one kid at a time will be responsible for the dishes. You might let one daughter do the dishes on Monday, Wednesday and Friday, and the other daughter do them on Tuesday, Thursday and Saturday, and mom will do them on Sunday. Likewise, it probably will be better for one daughter to have certain responsibilities, like setting the table, dusting, carrying out the trash, and the other daughter to be assigned to clearing the table, washing the windows, and walking the dog. That way there will be less chance of bickering and manipulation.

Bedtime for most families seems to be the biggest nuisance problem of all. I think for the most part it is the parents who have the problem of setting the limits and insisting bedtime is bedtime. Do not give in to that, "Oh, mom, can't I just stay up and watch the end of this program?" A nice solution consists of setting a bedtime, but not a sleeptime. Each kid should have a specific time at which he must leave the family and go to bed. There is no question or quibbling about that time and it is a hard and fast rule. You can make a kid go to bed, but you cannot make him go to sleep. Bugging him about going to sleep will just be a big source of hard feelings for the entire family. Once he is in bed, if he wants to leave his light on and read or go off to sleep, the choice is his. If it is handled in this way, he will rarely abuse the privilege. Reading not only helps him relax from the day's excitement, but most likely will help him be a better reader and learn to enjoy literature, a side benefit we should not pass up.

When it is necessary for kids to share a room there are frequently additional problems, such as playing and talking. Keep in mind that it takes two to talk. If one of the kids is tired and wants to go to sleep (and his parents stay out of the situation) it is likely that he will roll over and ignore the other one's talking. It is a good rule to insist that the kids need to stay in their own beds, but ignore their talking. The more you discourage talking, the more talking they will do.

Whether you are handling bedtime, chores, allowance or any other nuisance problems, do it in a way that will get the job done and minimize hard feelings.

CHAPTER XXVI

Parents' Rights

I am fed up with parents being maligned and criticized and, in short, being told they are solely responsible for all the troubles of the world. It is simply not true and I want to come to the defense of parents, not only because I am one, but because I feel they have been unfairly criticized for many years.

There is one fallacy that is held by many people; problem kids come from parents who do not care. Nothing could be farther from the truth. As a matter of fact, problem kids come from parents who probably care too much. These parents are not cruel and uncaring, it is just that sometimes caring makes them do things they later regret. *Problem kids come from parents who tend to overreact.* Let us look at why they overreact. It is not out of malice or cruelty. They themselves may have had a tough childhood and probably their own parents tended to overreact. But they also overreact because they love their children very much, and want them to grow up "right." When you look at it carefully, these parents' only crimes are caring too much and trying too hard. Are these really such terrible crimes? Most parents have a very deep and genuine desire to do everything they can for their kids. But that can be a double-edged sword. The parent who never takes a vacation so his kids can have the things they need will be frustrated (after all he needs his vacations too), and he will tend to get angry easily. And on whom does he take out his anger? You are right, the kid. This is a good example of how sometimes our good intentions go awry, and we end up hurting our kids when we really are only trying to help them. How about the parents who take on second jobs so they can provide better for their families? Their being away from home so much ends up being destructive to the family, rather than helpful. Again, the end result is the exact opposite of what the parents sought originally.

Perhaps in the frontier days parents needed to strive that hard to protect and to provide for their families; then it was a matter of survival. But let us face it, most of us do not have to eke out a living any more by scratching the ground. Our kids do not need us as much because we now have help from other institutions such as the school. *We*

180

have some rights as parents too. We have a right to live our own lives also. I have not preached neglect anywhere in this book nor am I preaching it now. But I am saying you have time to do a good job as a parent, and still enjoy your own life as well. We need to work hard to be good parents, but not too hard. We need to give our kids love, but we have a right to expect love for ourselves. You have enough time and energy to be a good parent, to have your own career, to have some time alone, and to be alone with your spouse. But you will only be able to appreciate these rights when you start demanding them. For years, many people have talked about giving the black man equal rights, but have not practiced that. It was only when the black man demanded his rights, that he started to fully realize them.

It troubles me deeply to see parents get "pushed around" by their kids. I have been in the homes of my friends and have seen their kids "running the show" (for example, the kids' dictating their own bedtime).

When I was in training I learned an expression from my chief, Doctor Finch, that goes something like this, "There are big people in the world, and little people in the world, and it's the big ones who tell the little one what to do." That is a very important statement. Unfortunately today in many families it is the other way around. Kids learn they can push their parents around, and having done that, they are ready for the bigger challenges, like the "Laws of the Land."

Parents have a right to be able to spend some time in the evening by themselves. The kids do not need to spend the entire evening in the living room watching TV, just because there are some interesting programs on. But that does happen when parents are unable to put their foot down and demand their rights. Even if the kids' bedtimes are later, they can still leave the living room at nine or ten o'clock so mom and dad can have some time alone together.

And how about mom and dad's time alone for sex? You have the right to enjoy sex with your spouse and yet how often parents tell me they cannot have sex anymore because they are afraid of their kid's walking in on them. The kid cannot walk in on you if the door is locked. Your bedroom should be a special place and the kids have no business being in there. I tell my kids that when my bedroom door is closed, they better not bother me unless they have a broken leg or the house is burning down. I cannot abuse that privilege either, by hiding in my bedroom from my responsibilities, or spending hours in there just to get away from the family.

Parents should have the right to go out in the evening. Kids are not supposed to be a ball and chain around your foot. And yet how many parents tell me they cannot go out because every time they try to leave their kid with a babysitter, he throws a "fit" or has a temper tantrum. Let him have his temper tantrums and his fits, but go out anyway. You need that time to yourselves.

I saw a couple recently who told me their four-year-old son called out repeatedly for several hours in the evening before going to sleep—"I want a glass of water. I want a glass of water." These parents went on to tell me how they could not get any rest in the evening because they kept jumping up and down to get their boy his many glasses of water. And yet when I asked them why they did that, they were stumped. They knew his body did not need the water, and they knew he was just manipulating them to stay up a little longer, but they were not insisting on their right as parents to have some peace and quiet in the evening. When they finally got up their courage and told their four-year-old that from then on he was going to have to get his own water, the problem disappeared.

How about all the parents who sacrifice throughout their lives so their kid can go to college? What happens then? These fine parents hand their kid his tuition, his books, his room and board, and his spending money and he goes off to college to have a ball. And after one or two semesters the parents are notified that their son has either been suspended for drugs or for protesting, or has flunked out because he has not been doing any academic work. What is obvious, then, is the parents are more interested in their son's college than he is. What about your kid's putting himself through college, either entirely alone or perhaps with a little assistance from you? It is not impossible. And what is more, he will work a lot harder while he is there, and he will probably appreciate it a lot more years later. I am sure you have had the same experience, but I look back with pride on the things I obtained for myself, much more than the things that were handed to me.

Parents' rights are something we give up all too easily. Perhaps they seem so insignificant we do not bother to fight for them, but I think they are important. For example, your right to use the toilet in privacy, or the right to take a bath without having the kids walk in. These are easily obtained, but only if you insist upon them. My wife and I have always felt we have a right to sleep late on Sunday mornings, so we have insisted on that right. As a matter of fact we have always slept late on Sunday mornings and the kids have learned to get up, get breakfast and take care of themselves. It has been an excellent experience for them in that it has added to their sense of responsibility.

I am not saying the world should revolve around parents, but I am also not saying the world should revolve around the kids either. There needs to be a compromise, a middle-ground in which both sides can satisfy their needs without neglecting the needs of the other. Sometimes parents can go out to dinner with their kids, and at other times just mom and dad. Sometimes the whole family can take a vacation and at other times just mom and dad should have a chance to be by themselves. The secret to a good family life is a healthy balance.

I would like to say a few words about working mothers, because I certainly feel mom has a right to a career of her own if she wishes. Some gals can find all the satisfaction they need in life by cooking, and cleaning, and raising their families and, in short, being good housewives and mothers. But that is not rewarding for many women. It does not give them the sense of accomplishment they need to be happy and to feel successful. That is not bad. Remember what I said before about different strokes for different folks? They should do the thing that allows them to feel worthwhile, that is to pursue a career as well as being a wife and mother. Many women do all three without ever neglecting their kids, their husbands, or their jobs.

There is a common fallacy I would like to correct. In raising your family, it is not the quantity of time you spend with them that is important, it is the quality. A recent book by Doctor Bruno Bettelheim, called *Children of the Dream,* nicely proves the point. The book is a graphic study of how Israeli kids grow up on a Kibbutz. Their parents only see the kids about two hours a day, and the rest of the day the children are in the care of specially trained teachers and nurses, and the parents are off at their jobs. Since this kind of system has been going on for over twenty-five years, Doctor Bettelheim was able to study the end product of such a system of childrearing. What was fascinating was that this system has produced a generation of kids almost entirely without many of the usual things that trouble us in our society. Delinquency, prostitution, homosexuality, and alcoholism, just to name a few, are almost completely nonexistent.

You see many mothers can be away from their families many hours a day and still transmit the needed love and attention. As a matter of fact, many mothers who work find it easier to love their kids in the few hours a day they are home, than they did when they were home twenty-four hours a day. The old traditions of dad's going to work and mom's staying home and cooking and cleaning are falling by the wayside, and appropriately so. Moms have a right and a need to have careers outside the home, if they wish. It is the quality not the quantity of time you spend with your kid that is important.

A family should not be a democracy. Mom and dad must listen to their kids' thoughts, opinions and feelings, but it is ultimately up to the "big people to tell the little people what to do."

CONCLUSION

After reading this book, if you have gotten the impression that kids, for the most part, are not born with problems, but many of the problems are created by parents, then you are doing just fine. Not a sense of blame or a sense of guilt, just the hard, cold realizations that you have the responsibility to handle thousands of situations with your kids; if you handle them correctly, the kids will grow up fine, and if you do not handle them correctly, there are going to be some problems. That is an awesome responsibility.

I make a lot of enemies when I talk like this, because parents do not want to face the fact that they have so many responsibilities for their kids. All too often I get the feeling that, when parents bring their kids to me as a psychiatrist, what the parents are really trying to do is to "drop off" their kid and pick him up when he is changed, almost as though they were dropping off a bundle of dirty laundry, expecting to pick it up when it is clean. I cannot change your kid, but you can—and you can do it by accepting the responsibility for him and making some effort *to change what you are doing first.*

I have also tried to show you in this book that just making the effort is not enough. After all, if I spend four hours digging a hole in the ground and the next four hours putting the dirt back, at the end of eight hours of hard work, I am going to have nothing to show for it. You must make the effort, but in the right direction. I think you are able to see how fighting a lot of unnecessary battles causes problems, and how creating a lot of hard feelings with your kids is going to hurt them. Many of us as parents put in a tremendous amount of effort, but in the wrong ways or over the wrong issues.

In finishing this book you have just completed the easy part—the theory. Now comes the tough part—applying it to yourselves and your family.

APPENDIX

ESSENTIAL DIFFERENCES BETWEEN THE THREE AGE GROUPS

	Children	Adolescents	Adults
Relationship to authority figures	Dependent	Working toward independence	Independent
Way of expressing feelings and re-solving conflicts	Play	Acting-out behavior	Verbally and intellectually
Source of values	Parents	Peers	Society
What they struggle with	Parents and need satisfaction	Fear of loss of con-trol of sexual and aggressive drives	Society
Emotional State	Growing	Disrupted	Growing
Sense of identity (Who am I?)	Naively clear	Disrupted	Reasonably Clear
Thinks about	Himself	Himself with respect to others	Others
Desire to move ahead	None (timelessness)	Intense in all di-rections	Slow and cautious
Curiosity	Mild	Intense	Minimal
Trust and faith in authority	Complete	"Paranoid" (untrusting)	Cautious